The Way of Forgiveness

Readings for a Peaceful Life

The Way of Forgiveness

Readings for a Peaceful Life

Michael Leach, James T. Keane, Doris Goodnough, editors

ORBIS BOOKS
Maryknoll, New York 10545

Maryknoll, New York 10545

Founded in 1970, Orbis Books endeavors to publish works that enlighten the mind, nourish the spirit, and challenge the conscience. The publishing arm of the Maryknoll Fathers and Brothers, Orbis seeks to explore the global dimensions of the Christian faith and mission, to invite dialogue with diverse cultures and religious traditions, and to serve the cause of reconciliation and peace. The books published reflect the views of their authors and do not represent the official position of the Maryknoll Society. To learn more about Maryknoll and Orbis Books, please visit our website at www.maryknollsociety.org.

Published by Orbis Books, Maryknoll, New York 10545-0302.

Manufactured in the United States of America.
Design: Roberta Savage

Library of Congress Cataloging-in-Publication Data
Names: Leach, Michael, 1940- editor.
Title: The way of forgiveness : readings for a peaceful life / Michael Leach,
James T. Keane, Doris Goodnough, editors.
Description: Maryknoll : Orbis Books, 2019. | Includes bibliographical references and index.
Identifiers: LCCN 2018050207 | ISBN 9781626983229 (pbk.)
Subjects: LCSH: Forgiveness—Religious aspects—Christianity. | Forgiveness.
Classification: LCC BV4647.F55 W39 2019 | DDC 241/.4—dc23 LC record available at https://lccn.loc.gov/2018050207

"There is no love without forgiveness,
and there is no forgiveness without love."

—Bryant H. McGill

Contents

Part Two
FORGIVING OTHERS
Seventy Times Seven
Matthew 18:21

Contents

Part Three
THE FORGIVENESS OF GOD

The Lord Is Merciful and Gracious
Psalm 103:8–12

The Way of Forgiveness

Contents

Introduction

The Way of Forgiveness is the third in a series of writings on values that transform us. First was *The Way of Gratitude*. Then *The Way of Kindness*. Our bet is that gratitude, kindness, and forgiveness are among the values you value most. The idea for the series is to share inspiring stories, from writers you love and writers you will love, that illuminate the power of these virtues to bring you freedom, joy, and peace.

The Way of Forgiveness features more than forty essays, stories, poems, and meditations on the rewards of forgiving and being forgiven (they often come at once) from Anne Lamott, Mary Oliver, e. e. cummings, Frederick Buechner, Joyce Rupp, James Martin, Maya Angelou, Richard Rohr, Marianne Williamson, Jon Mundy, Jack Kornfield, Dorothy Day, C. S. Lewis, and many others. You could do worse than invite any of these folk to your house to sit around the kitchen table and have a cup of coffee and talk about life or anything at all. This book also intersperses wisdom from the likes of Shakespeare, Oprah, and The Little Prince, and texts from Buddhism, Judaism, Christianity, and Islam. Here is a fun quote from Erma Bombeck: "People are always asking couples whose marriages have endured at least a quarter of a century for their secret of success. Actually, it's no secret at all. I am a forgiving woman. Long ago, I forgave my husband for not being Paul Newman." Hey, let's reach to heaven and invite Erma and Paul to the kitchen table too! Open the window and let the sun shine in!

Can you imagine a world without the lightness of forgiveness? How could anyone go on? We all need to stop blaming ourselves and others, and lay our resentments on the altar of consciousness, saying, "Please, God, take these thoughts away from me. They are my crown of thorns and they hurt so much. Give me *your* thoughts. Think for me. Your thoughts only!" And soon we will hear, and soon we will whisper, "God, forgive them, for they know not what they do." And night shall be day, and we shall be well for we shall know forgiveness too.

The purpose of *The Way of Forgiveness* is to let the sun shine in your soul. "There is a crack in everything," Leonard Cohen sang, "that's how the light gets in." Forgiveness is warm, it heals the cracks in even the most hardened hearts. It is strong, it lasts.

It is forever, even if it takes seventy times seven times to get it right. And most of all, forgiveness is from God—it will set you free.

Michael Leach, James T. Keane, Doris Goodnough

Part One
FORGIVING YOURSELF

Neither Do I Condemn You

John 8:2–11

The scribes and the Pharisees brought a woman who had been caught in adultery; and making her stand before all of them, they said to Jesus, “Teacher, this woman was caught in the very act of committing adultery. Now in the law Moses commanded us to stone such women. Now what do you say?” They said this to test him, so that they might have some charge to bring against him. Jesus bent down and wrote with his finger on the ground. When they kept on questioning him, he straightened up and said to them, “Let anyone among you who is without sin be the first to throw a stone at her.” And once again he bent down and wrote on the ground. When they heard it, they went away, one by one, beginning with the elders; and Jesus was left alone with the woman standing before him. Jesus straightened up and said to her, "Woman, where are they? Has no one condemned you?" She said, "No one, sir." And Jesus said, "Neither do I condemn you. Go your way, and from now on do not sin again."

1

The Gentle Gift of Mercy

Anne Lamott

There are times in our lives—scary, unsettling times—when we know that we need help or answers but we're not sure what kind, or even what the problem or question is. We look and look, tearing apart our lives like we're searching for car keys in our couch, and we come up empty-handed. Then when we're doing something stupid, like staring at the dog's mismatched paws, we stumble across what we needed to find. Or even better, it finds us.

It wasn't what we were looking or hoping for, which was usually advice, approval, an advantage, safety or relief from pain. I was raised to seek or achieve them, but like everyone, I realized at some point that they do not bring lasting peace, relief or uplift. This does not seem fair, after a lifetime spent in their pursuit.

Where, then, do I turn in these increasingly frightening days? Where do I look for answers when I'm afraid, or confused, or numb? To an elegant Japanese sage? A dream-dancing Sioux grandmother with a tinkling laugh? No. More often than not, the North Star that guides me through the darkness is the Old Testament prophet Micah. He must have looked like a complete stoner or a Game of Thrones extra, and smelled like a goat, yet nearly three thousand years ago, he spoke the words that often remind me of my path and purpose: "What doth God require of thee but to do justice and to love mercy, and to walk humbly with thy God?"

Oh, is that all? Justice, mercy, and humility? That's nice. Right off the bat I can tell you that "walk humbly with thy God" is not going to happen anytime soon, for me or my closest friends—Arrogance R Us. My humility can kick your humility's butt. What Micah is talking about is grad-school curriculum, while, spiritually speaking, I remain in junior high school, superior and cringing at the same time. And "to do justice" may be a trick, since we all think we do this anyway. We think that if our values aren't the correct ones, we would have other ones, which would then be the correct ones.

Otherwise, these words are both plainsong and sublime. How can you not love mercy—kindness, compassion, forgiveness? It's like not loving dessert, or cheese. If nothing makes people happier than service, especially to the poor, why not tap into the model of the Buddha, Jesus, or Wavy Gravy, the knowledge that if you do loving things, you'll have loving feelings?

Just to hear the words "mercy" or "merciful" can transform the whole day, because as the old saying goes, the soul rejoices in hearing what it already knows. Something lights up in me. We know mercy is always our salvation—as we age, as our grandchildren go down the same dark streets that called to their parents, as the ice caps melt. But I wish it was something else. I wish it was being able to figure things out, at which I am very good, or to assign blame, at which I am better, or to convince people of the rightness of my ideas. I wish it was a political savior who believes the same things I believe, who possesses the force of great moral strength that (of course) agrees with my own deepest values. But no, hope of renewal and restoration is found in the merciful fibrillating heart of the world.

Maybe it would be helpful to ask what we mean when we speak or dream of mercy. Here, off the top of my head, in no particular order, are several things of which I am fairly sure.

Mercy is radical kindness. Mercy means offering or being offered aid in desperate straits. Mercy is not deserved. It involves absolving the unabsolvable, forgiving the unforgivable. Mercy brings us to the miracle of apology, given and accepted, to unashamed humility when we have erred or forgotten. Charge it to our heads and not our hearts, as the elders in black churches have long said.

Mercy, grace, forgiveness, and compassion are synonyms, and the approaches we might consider taking when facing a great big mess, especially the great big mess of ourselves—our arrogance, greed, poverty, disease, prejudice. It includes everything out there that just makes us sick and makes us want to turn away, the idea of accepting life as it presents itself and doing goodness anyway, the belief that love and caring are marbled even into the worst life has to offer.

In many spiritual and wisdom paths, it is written that God created us to have company and to be God's loving eyes and hands on earth. But in certain African Christian catechisms it says that God created us because He thought we would like it. This stops me in my tracks. We would like it?

Yes, of course we like the friendly, warm or breathtaking parts of life. But it's so hard for almost everyone here, the whole world over, let alone my own beloved. You cannot believe what the people I love most have lost this year. God thought we would like puberty, warfare, and snakes? I could go on and on—senescence, global warming, Parkinson's, spiders?

Yes, because in the words of Candi Staton's great gospel song "Hallelujah Anyway" Hallelujah that in spite of it all, there is love, there is singing, nature, laughing, mercy.

Mercy means that we soften ever so slightly, so that we don't have to condemn others for being total shits, although they may be that. (Okay: are.) If I do so, it makes me one. As Father Ed Dowling said, sometimes heaven is just a new pair of glasses. When we put them on, we see the awful person, sometimes even ourselves, a bit more gently, and we are blessed in return. It seems, on the face of things, like a decent deal.

Kindness toward others and radical kindness to ourselves buy us a shot at a warm and generous heart, which is the greatest prize of all. Do you want this, or do you want to be right? Well, can I get back to you on that? I want to want this softening, this surrender, this happiness. Can I get a partial credit for that?

The good news is that God has such low standards, and reaches out to those of us who are often not lovable and offers us a chance to come back in from the storm of drama and toxic thoughts. Augustine wrote, "Late have I loved you, o beauty ever ancient. . . . You were within me but I was outside." The storm outside is just so much more enlivening, and for a writer, much better material. Plus, I can be a hero in my storm, which is where I found a sense of value as a child, as the tense little EMT in a damaged family. Crisis, self-centered fear, and saving people were home for me, with a wet bar serving up adrenaline. The quiet, tranquil room of just being was boarded up. But love reaches out and reaches out and reaches out. It is staggering that it is always giving me another chance, another day, over and over and over.

When we manage a flash of mercy for someone we don't like, especially a truly awful person, including ourselves, we experience a great spiritual moment, a new point of view that can make us gasp. It gives us the chance to rediscover something both old and original, the sweet child in us who, all evidence to the contrary, was not killed off, but just put in the drawer. I realize now how desperately, how grievously, I have needed the necessary mercy to experience self-respect.

It is what a lot of us were so frantic for all along, and we never knew it. We've tried almost suicidally for our whole lives to shake it from the boughs of the material world's trees. But it comes from within, from love, from the flow of the universe; from inside the cluttered drawer.

My unloveliness, on the other hand, is always on tap, like draft beer—my boring self-obsession, pettiness, and schadenfreude. Wearing my bad pair of glasses, I look around and see that I am surrounded by swine. How do you expect me to react? But God, in Her guise as Coyote Trickster, gooses me, and I accidentally let go. I take a break from being prickly and judgmental.

I stop, pull back, take a breath. The next thing I know, I let others go first, or see that perhaps now is not the time to demand an explanation or an apology. Against all odds, I'll somehow stop the campaign for now. I start over. I'm able to keep the patient more patient. And I get me back. What's the catch? The catch is that there is no catch. This is so subversive. All I have to do in order to begin again is to love mercy, if I am to believe nutty old Micah. Then creation begins to float by, each new day.

2

Forgiveness Repairs the World

Jack Kornfield

Buddhist psychology offers specific teachings and practices for the development of forgiveness. Like the practice of compassion, forgiveness does not ignore the truth of our suffering. Forgiveness is not weak. It demands courage and integrity. Yet only forgiveness and love can bring about the peace we long for. As the Indian sage Meher Baba explains, "True love is not for the faint-hearted."

We have all betrayed and hurt others, just as we have knowingly or unknowingly been harmed by them. It is inevitable in this human realm. Sometimes our betrayals are small, sometimes terrible. Extending and receiving forgiveness is essential for redemption from our past. To forgive does not mean we condone the misdeeds of another. We can dedicate ourselves to make sure they never happen again. But without forgiveness the world can never be released from the sorrows of the past. Someone quipped, "Forgiveness means giving up all hope for a better past." Forgiveness is a way to move on.

In Buddhist psychology, forgiveness is not presented as a moral commandment; thou shalt forgive. It is understood as a way to end suffering, to bring dignity and harmony to our life. Forgiveness is fundamentally for our own sake, for our own mental health. It is a way to let go of the pain we carry. This is illustrated by the story of two ex-prisoners of war who meet after many years. When the first one asks, "Have you forgiven your captors yet?" the second man answers, "No, never." "Well then," the first man replies, "they still have you in prison." For most people, the work of forgiveness is a process. Practicing forgiveness, we may go through stages of grief, rage, sorrow, fear, and confusion. As we let ourself feel the pain we still hold, forgiveness comes as a relief, a release for our heart in the end. Forgiveness acknowledges that no matter how much we may have suffered, we will not put another human being out of our heart.

The practice of forgiveness grows through generosity and repetition. One of my teachers instructed me to practice five minutes of forgiveness for myself and others, twice a day for six months, which meant 360 times. Practicing with small misdeeds, such as my uncaring treatment of a friend, I repeatedly asked her forgiveness and gradually forgave myself. That experience encouraged me, but when I turned to my father, the process was much more difficult. Forgiveness took many years. It was only when he lay dying that I could look back and reflect on what had released me from our family suffering. When, at age 75, ten years after his first heart attack, my father was near death from congestive heart failure, frightened and in pain, I sat with him over long days and late nights. He kept asking me to stay. Because I had sat with my own pain and fear in meditation, I was not afraid. Because I had sat in the charnel grounds and with others as they died, I was able to offer the steady presence he needed. By now I also knew enough not to blurt out that I loved him, but I also knew that he could feel that I did.

Years of meditation, therapy, and forgiveness practices had come with me into that room. I'd worked with my rage at my father and my sorrow and frustration as a frightened, impotent child. One day I pictured the yellow linoleum floor in the backroom where my father was beating my mother. I wanted to beat him and to rescue her. I felt sorry for and angry at my mother for her weakness, and for her collusion with his brutal arrogance. I struggled to release my father and all his rigid, paranoid violence. I relived the nighttime scenes where his eyes would become glazed and crazed looking, and the old bastard would curse and hit and hurt us, his family.

As I meditated and wept, I felt the pain of my own closed heart and wondered how I could forgive him. I breathed and practiced forgiveness and got inside his own wretched history, and my mother's paralyzing fear. I saw him as a young teen when his father died. My father and his father were both caught between two women who hated each other. His coldly polished and controlling mother and his tight-fisted and iron-willed grandmother who lived just across the street and ran the family business. I saw his paranoia and fear and how hard his uncontrollable rage must have been for him. I saw his inexcusable acts and his unmanageable pain. It helped when I discovered that my own rage was not so different from his. I learned to respect the anger, depression, cynicism, and humor that my brothers and I had used to survive. I saw that we were not alone. I felt connected to a million fathers and estranged sons, to generations of family wounds, many greater than my own. Then I gradually saw, too, his creative and loving side, along with his capacity to hurt those he loved, and finally his humanity, all our humanity. And in the last days in the hospital, I could sit with him in all his complexity and forgive.

When students come to Buddhist practice, they learn the blessings of the path of forgiveness. Josh's half brothers had legally cheated him out of part of his inheritance. He knew that through his own inattention he was complicit as well. Over five years he had tried to straighten things out with them, with only a little success. Still he carried the suffering and betrayal like a weight in his body. He had not been a regular meditator but to release his suffering, he undertook a systematic forgiveness practice. He knew that finding compassion and forgiveness were crucial for his well-being. At first he struggled, and whenever his bitterness arose, I suggested he pay attention to his body. He could feel a familiar block of rigid tension in his shoulders and upper arms and a constricted pain in his chest. The clenched hurt and anger were a painful sign. He didn't want to live this way. Even though he didn't get the money, he did not want to live hating his brothers. Josh knew he had to release them. Over several months of repeated practice, the spirit of forgiveness came in, and little by little he learned to let go.

Forgiveness was also important for Julie, a college biosciences professor who worked as an ecological activist in Brazil and Guatemala. On retreat she told me how she had recently seduced a graduate student, and two young women in the field. She had mixed her love needs with the good work she was doing and her activism became a kind of self-justification for these relationships. It all came up in her meditation. Julie was not sorry for her attempts at love and connection, but she deeply regretted the pain and betrayal she had caused.

I suggested that Julie write the whole set of stories down. They poured out of her. Then I asked her permission to read them. She gave them to me, and when I had done so we met together. I asked her what she felt we should do next. Her eyes watered and she said she wanted to ask forgiveness. I offered her my own, and told her that she had to consciously understand and feel the impact of her actions to commit to not harming. She thought she would write to these women. Then she had to find a way to forgive herself so she could be released from the past and let it go.

Even in extreme cases, the Buddhist teachings counsel forgiveness. In the Dhammapada, the Buddha gives an instruction that is both fierce and compassionate. "If someone has abused you, beat you, robbed you, abandon your thoughts of anger. Soon you will die. Life is too short to live with hatred." With forgiveness we become unwilling to wish harm to another. Whenever we forgive, in small ways at home, or in great ways between nations, we free ourselves from the past. This is necessary for the Bosnians and Serbs, the Irish Catholics and Protestants, the Hutus and Tutsis. It is necessary to us all to find ways to forgive.

Laura grew up with a lot of shame about being poor. Outwardly she tried to overcome this by hard work. Laura was the first in her extended family to go to college, struggling with feeling insecure, like an outcast. After she graduated, she worked in the city for the Department of Public Safety. Sixteen years later she transferred to a farming community just in from the coast near Oxnard. She said, "Now that I've lived in the city, when I go into the coffee shop and see the old clothes, the uneducated farmers, it's so easy to judge them and feel myself as different. We may be different in education and politics, but these are false ways we separate ourselves. Then when I really look, I just want to drop my judgments and be with them, with us."

"My father was like them. He drank too much. He berated us, his daughters. He was terrible to his sons. I was desperate to get free of him, of our family. But my shame, anger, and resentment stayed with me. When I began Buddhist practice, it was hard to sit still. After a while I realized how sad I was, how much hurt was in my body. I was just trying to cope. I was grateful to be taught the loving-kindness and forgiveness practices. I did them twice a day for two years. I needed to forgive myself for being so angry and ashamed, as much as to forgive my father. Practicing forgiveness was like learning to stand and walk and feel good about myself. Then I was able to go home, to see my family, even my father, without hurting so much. Seven years later when my father got sick, it wasn't hard to go back. I saw his slow decline until finally he was a weak old man on his bed. I knew that I loved him. I had forgiven us all." With virtue and forgiveness we repair the world.

Mercies

Let us forgive each other—only then will we live in peace.

—Leo Tolstoy

When a deep injury is done to us, we never heal until we forgive.

—Nelson Mandela

Forgiveness is the answer to the child's dream of a miracle by which what is broken is made whole again, what is soiled is made clean again.

—Dag Hammarskjold

3

A Settlement

Mary Oliver

Look, it's spring. And last year's loose dust has turned into this soft willingness. The wind-flowers have come up trembling, slowly the brackens are up-lifting their curvaceous and pale bodies. The thrushes have come home, none less than filled with mystery, sorrow, happiness, music, ambition.

And I am walking out into all of this with nowhere to go and no task undertaken but to turn the pages of this beautiful world over and over, in the world of my mind.

⋄⋄⋄

Therefore, dark past,
I'm about to do it.
I'm about to forgive you
for everything.

4

The Key to Happiness

Jon Mundy

False Forgiveness

A Sunday School teacher asked her class what we must do before we can be forgiven of our sin, expecting someone to say that we must repent of our sin. One young man reached back even further and said, "First you must sin." This is the gist of *A Course in Miracles.* The Course takes the radical view that we have never sinned at all. Therefore, there is nothing to forgive. How is this possible? The world is full of murders, betrayals, thievery, and other terrible sins. This chapter will explain how A Course in Miracles views the world and these seeming sins.

Someone once said, "No one forgets where the hatchet is buried." We sometimes hear people say, "I can forgive but I cannot forget." We can each probably think of times when something we thought was long forgotten and well-buried is very much the topic of conversation, "What you did in 2008, when you lost all our money on that horrible investment." It has not been forgotten, so it has not been forgiven. "I can forgive but I cannot forget," is only another way of saying, "I will not forgive."

The ego's plan is to have you see error clearly first,
then overlook it, yet how can you overlook what you have made real?
By seeing it clearly,
you have made it real and cannot overlook it.

(Chapter 9, IV.4:4–6)*

The ego experiences sin by placing itself in a "holier-than-thou" position from which others may be forgiven for the wrong we think they have done. By witnessing sin, we provide testimony to its reality. We cannot forgive a sin we believe is real. True forgiveness requires a complete reversal in thinking. We need a perspective outside the realm of the ego. The ego version of forgiveness is, thus, not forgiveness but judgment masquerading as forgiveness. We cannot then overlook what we make real. In fact, the more clearly we see error, the more we make it real, and the less we are able to overlook it.

The following is a dialogue between a husband and a wife:

Husband: "Why do you keep bringing up my past mistakes? I thought you had forgiven and forgotten."

Wife: "I have, indeed, forgiven and forgotten, but I don't want you to forget that I forgave and forgot."

We may offer pardon sometimes but we retain the awareness that the offender has sinned. This process keeps sin alive. The Course asks us to look beyond the appearance. This is admittedly not easy to do and a great "struggle" while we remain trapped in the ego perspective. Convinced of the reality of "sin" in our brother, it is impossible to see the face of Christ within.

Just before Leonardo da Vinci commenced work on his *Last Supper*, he had a quarrel with a fellow painter. Leonardo was so enraged and bitter that he was determined to paint the face of his enemy, the other artist, into the face of Judas. Thus would he take his revenge and "vent his spleen," handing the man

---

* Notations appearing at the end of quotations reference the location of the various quotes and paraphrases from the source book *A Course in Miracles*, 2nd ed. (Glen Ellen, CA: The Foundation for Inner Peace, 1992).

down in infamy and scorn to succeeding generations. The face of Judas was the first that he finished, and everyone could see it was the face of the painter with whom he had quarreled. When Leonardo came to paint the face of Jesus, he couldn't do it. Something was thwarting his best efforts. Eventually, he painted out the face of Judas and commenced anew on the face of Jesus, this time with success.

We cannot paint the features of Christ into our own life and at the same time paint a brother's face with the colors of enmity and hatred. When we cannot forgive, we cannot see peace. The statement: "May God forgive you your sins" is a strange parody. A loving Father cannot bring condemnation upon us. God cannot forgive sin because God does not condemn (Lesson 46, 1:1). In order to have forgiveness, we must first have condemnation. There is no forgiveness in Heaven because it's not needed.

There is a story about a Catholic priest who lived in the Philippines, a much-loved man who carried a burden of guilt about a long past sin. He had committed this so-called sin many years before, during his time in seminary. No one knew of it. There was a woman in his parish who claimed she regularly spoke with the Holy Spirit. The priest was, of course, skeptical about her claim so he said: "The next time you talk to the Holy Spirit, ask him what sin it was your priest committed while he was in seminary."

The woman agreed and went home. When she returned to church a few days later, the priest said, "Did you ask the Holy Spirit what sin your priest committed in seminary?"

"Yes," the woman said, "I asked him."

"Well," said the priest, "What did he say?"

The woman responded: "He said, 'I don't remember.'"

That is the right answer because the Holy Spirit does not make sin real or seek to compound error. God does not engage in reprisal. God does not know about illusion. We may understand this best in the love we have for our children, when we forgive regardless of what seems to have happened. The past is always the past and can have no effect on the present.

My friend Rabbi Joseph Gelberman escaped Hitler's growing terror and fled to the United States in 1939, with plans of bringing along his wife, daughter, mother, father, brothers, and sisters. Two of his brothers also made it to the United States. Everyone else died in the concentration camps, including his wife and daughter. Joseph said his hatred for Hitler was so great, that he finally realized that unless he could rise above it and forgive the whole insanity Hitler was going to wind up killing him too. It took many years for him to do so and it tried his faith, 'til one day he realized that in order for peace to return to his own mind he was going to have to let it go and forgive. As I write this, he is now 97.

Sometimes when I'm asked, "How can I possibly forgive...," I respond, "If you want peace of mind, you don't have any choice, someday you're going to let it go, so you might as well let it go now." As the Course expresses it, "Why wait for Heaven?" (Lesson 131, 6:1).

Forgiveness Is a Reciprocal Process

As we extend forgiveness, so are we forgiven. The Lord's Prayer says, "Forgive us our debts," then there is the very important word, 'as' "we forgive our debtors." As giving is a preface to receiving, and judging is a preface to being judged, so forgiveness prefaces our experience of being forgiven. There is nothing to forgive, unless we believe there is. As we forgive by not condemning, we are freed of suffering. In this process, we are healed. As we give, we receive; as we forgive (by not making the error real), so are we forgiven; as we forgive, so do we remember our heavenly home.

During the Korean War, a South Korean civilian was arrested by the communists and ordered shot. But when the young communist leader learned that the prisoner was in charge of an orphanage, he decided to spare him and to kill the South Korean civilian's son instead. So they shot the nineteen-year-old boy in the presence of the father. Later, the fortunes of war changed, and the young communist leader was captured by the United Nations' forces, tried, and condemned to death. But before the sentence could be carried out, the South Korean, whose son had been killed, pleaded for the life of the communist, saying: "He was young. He did not know what he was doing." The United Nations' forces granted his request; and the South Korean civilian took his son's murderer into his own home.

While God sees no differences among illusions, we certainly do, and forgiving the murder of one's child is about as tough as it comes. Without the love of God in our hearts, it is impossible to forgive. The South Korean man was filled with that love and it was this which enabled his response. He saw that the murderer was acting insanely and did not know what he was doing. When someone is insane, they need our help, not our attack.

There Is No Future in the Past

To make sin real and then try to forgive it affirms its reality. Our pardon is then a useless attempt to overlook what we think is true. If we make an illusion real, the pardon we offer the world is a deception. We don't really forgive, and we show that we do not, by hanging on to our hurt feelings. The major problem we have in relationship to forgiveness is that we believe we must forgive the truth and not an illusion. If we think that an offense is real, we must then also believe that forgiveness is a lie (Lesson 134 3:1, 4:2). We demonstrate our knowledge of Heaven by showing others that their so-called sins have not affected us.

This is what Jesus is doing on the cross. It did not matter what they were doing to his body. He knew he was not a body. We overlook mistakes by giving them no effect. Not being affected by "*sin*," we remove its cause. Jesus did not condemn those who crucified him. Our task is no different than his. We are to teach no one that they can hurt us (T.14, 3, 8:7). Another way to say this is that time cannot intrude upon eternity—the unreal cannot affect the real. The ego lives in time, constantly rehearsing the past and projecting the future. If there is no past, there is nothing to hang on to. There is nothing to project on to; there is just this moment and there is nothing to forgive in the moment. As a popular country western song once expressed it: "There is no future in the past."

Forgiveness does not keep time. It ends it. There must literally be no past to hang on to. When missionaries first went to Labrador, they found that the Eskimos had no word for forgiveness. So they made up a word, which in Eskimo was: Is-suma-gi-jou-jung-naimer-mik which meant, "Not-being-able-to-think-about-it-any-more."

A missionary asked a young Eskimo girl if she had made her peace with God and she replied, "I did not know there was any quarrel. In a similar way, Henry David Thoreau on his deathbed was asked by one of his aunts if he had made his peace with God and he said, "We never argued." Bill Thetford, Helen's companion in the composition of the Course, was once asked how one could know if they were advancing in the Course and he said, "You know by how long you hold a grievance."

The sooner we let it go the better and if we're

Christlike in our consciousness, we don't get attached to it to start with. In the story of the woman taken in adultery, the disciples are amazed that Jesus does not see the woman in question as they do; namely, someone with an unsavory reputation.

When you bury a mad dog, don't leave his tail above ground.

—Charles Spurgeon

The past is the past. What is done is done even if it just happened a minute ago. To forgive means to let it all go—to hold on to nothing. As we forgive by not condemning, we are freed of suffering. In the realm of the ego, no one forgets where the hatchet is buried. We may pretend that we have forgiven, but we cannot forgive a sin we believe is real.

Unjustified forgiveness is attack.
And this is all the world can ever give.
It pardons "sinners" sometimes,
but remains aware that they have sinned.
And so they do not merit the forgiveness that it gives.
This is the false forgiveness
which the world employs to keep the sense of sin alive.

(Chapter 30, VI. 3:5–8 & 4:1)

To witness sin and then try to forgive it is backward thinking. Concentration on error is only further error. We demonstrate our knowledge of Heaven by showing others that their transgressions against us do not have an effect. We can demonstrate, as Jesus did, that we cannot be betrayed. It is not difficult to overlook mistakes once we do not give them any effect over us (T-30.VI.10:2). By not being affected by "sin," we remove its cause. Jesus did not condemn those who crucified him. Our task is no different than his. There is no death, and this we demonstrate by showing that we cannot be hurt.

The major difficulty that you find in genuine
forgiveness on your part is
that you still believe you must forgive the truth
and not illusions.
For it is impossible to think of sin as true and
not believe forgiveness is a lie.

Workbook Lesson 134, 3:1 and 4:2

The task is to let go so completely that there is no memory of wrong-doing, because there is nothing in us to make things wrong. When faced with attack, criticism, and condemnation, it is helpful to realize that all attack is a call for help. All fear is a call for love. If we think that someone has mistreated us, rather than jumping to a defense, can we not realize that that person has acted out of fear and ignorance?

Can we not see mistakes as a call for help?

. . . you are merely asked to see forgiveness
as the natural reaction to distress that rests on error,
and thus calls for help.
Forgiveness is the only sane response.
(Chapter 30, VI. 2:7–8)

Have I Done What I'm Accusing the Other of Doing?

Whenever we feel tempted to accuse someone of being a sinner, it is helpful to ask ourselves if what that person has done is something we would accuse ourselves of doing. In the story of the woman taken in adultery, Jesus suggests that the one who is without sin should cast the first stone. Beginning with the eldest, they drop their stones and walk away. Jesus then turns to the woman and asks, "Woman, where are your accusers?" to which she says, "Lord, there are none." Jesus then replies, "Neither do I condemn you; go and sin no more." In other words, "go and do not continue to make the same mistake." It is the eldest who drops the first stone. The deeper we go in examining our own consciousness, the more we've been here, the more we know we have not been able to transition through this world without error.

Everyone to whom we offer healing returns it. Everyone we attack holds it against us. The cost of giving is always receiving. God is the only Cause and God does not cause guilt. What is not of God cannot have power over us (T-14.III.8:1f). We would never attack another unless we believed that that person had somehow taken the peace of God from us. But no one can take the peace of God from us unless we give them that power.

Forgiveness Must Be Total

Then Peter went up to him and said,
"Lord, how often must I forgive my brother if he wrongs me? As often as seven times?"
Jesus answered, "Not seven, I tell you, but seventy times seven."

Matthew 8:21–22

We cannot forgive some people and not forgive others. There cannot be some things we forgive in someone but other things about that same person we cannot forgive. Forgiveness is not something we do sometimes. To forgive "seventy times seven" means to forgive repeatedly—infinitely, no matter how wrong we might think another has been, no matter how many times we may think we have been abused. The answer remains:

"Forgive," "Forgive," "Forgive."
"Let it go," "Let it go," "Let it go."

Peace is obtainable when we hold to these ideas:

1. Peace of mind, salvation, and the abundance that comes with it can be our only goal.

2. Through forgiveness, we begin to see everyone, including ourselves, as guiltless. If Jesus, on the cross, can forgive murderers, can we not be more tolerant of lesser sins that we think have been committed against us?

3. As we give up our grievances, we find ourselves becoming increasingly aware of the ever-present, subtle, and gentle guidance of Holy Spirit.

Following Holy Spirit, we do not condemn others. It is then that we can experience peace of mind. With Holy Spirit's guidance, it becomes possible to know what we are supposed to do and do it.

As long as we are unforgiving, we can justify the belief that whatever is wrong in the world is caused by something or someone that is outside of us or other than us.

As long as we think there is something we cannot forgive, we block our own way to the Kingdom.

As long as we project guilt and sin upon the world, we ourselves live in confusion and despair.

As long as we live in fear, love has no place in our hearts.

A Practical Test for Forgiveness

There is a very practical test to see if we have forgiven. If I truly do it, I come to a realization— "I am the one who is forgiven. I am the one who is liberated. I am the one who is now free. It never did have anything to do with the other. What I am letting go of is my own condemnation." This does not mean that the other may not have done something in the world. The world is full of examples of one brother hurting another. It is also full of miracles. Indeed, most miracles remain unseen. How many acts of forgiveness have occurred about which no one knows anything? There is nothing to fear. No one can take anything from us. To be alive, free, and at peace—forgive. As we forgive, we come to know ourselves the way God created us. Only as we forgive, do we experience the Kingdom of Heaven.

Society cannot permit murder, rape, or other assaults by one body upon others. We lock such folks away because we do not know what else to do. Throughout the 1980s, I worked as a college lecturer inside both Sing Sing and Bedford Prison for Women, in New York State. There is a sign outside the gate at Sing Sing which says, "Sing Sing, New York State Correctional Institution." It would be nice to think that this is a place of correction. I taught for over 40 years and in that time, I only gave one A+. The woman who earned it was a student in Bedford Prison. Lisa was an absolute delight. She sat in the front row and was obviously quite bright. She was also funny. We would often do little forms of "intellectual sparking" with each other over various ideas. She earned the A+ because she was the only student I ever had who not only read the text book—she also read every book she could get her hands on in the bibliography at the end of the text.

We teachers were not to inquire after our students' crimes. If a student voluntarily told you their crime, that was one thing, but we were not to ask. One evening, I was leaving the prison with another teacher and I asked her if she had Lisa as a student and then said, "Isn't she the most wonderful student? She is an absolute joy." And the other teacher, said, "Yes, you know her crime, don't you? She drowned her daughter in the bath tub." I did not know. What if I had known her crime before the class began? Would I have come to appreciate, even admire her as much as I did? While working in prison, I got to know many wonderful students as human beings. They made what we would think of as some big mistakes, otherwise they could not have been there; but I got to know them as people not as criminals. Regardless of the egregious nature of our crimes, we are all just people here.

All Forgiveness Is Self-Forgiveness

As sin is an idea you taught yourself, forgiveness must be learned by you
as well, but from a Teacher other than yourself, who represents the other Self in you.
Through Him you learn how to forgive the self you think you made, and let it disappear.
Thus you return your mind as one to Him Who is your Self, and Who can never sin.

(Lesson 121, 6:3–5)

Ultimately, there is no one to forgive but ourselves and what we forgive ourselves for is our own misperceptions. We can use a capital 'S' when talking about

Self-forgiveness, as we are only capable of forgiving ourselves from a higher point of view. We cannot forgive from the ego's perspective. As the ego's very nature is hatred and separation, it cannot possibly forgive. Therefore, true forgiveness is prefaced by Self-realization. As we forgive, so are we forgiven. To forgive is to overlook, to relinquish the past, to let go of everything, to hold on to nothing. In the deepest sense, to forgive means to forget—to forget where the hatchet is buried, to let it go to another time, and go on.

How to Forgive

- Experience the anger. Look at what you think your brother has done. Don't deny or repress it. Don't throw it out onto another—don't attack physically or verbally. Feel it fully, you are really mad.
- Own your feelings. The Course is about being responsible. No one can "make us" feel, believe, or act in any way. No one can really "make us" feel angry.
- Give your anger to the Holy Spirit for correc tion. "Holy Spirit, I have done this thing (get ting angry) to myself and it is this I would undo."
- Thank the Holy Spirit for His help in forgive ness. This is how love is shared.

Forgiveness Itself Is an Illusion

It may sound funny having said so much about forgiveness to now say that forgiveness itself is an illusion. It is an illusion because there is nothing to forgive in the first place. There is something to forgive only if "we think" there is something to forgive.

Illusions make illusion. Except one.
Forgiveness is illusion that is answer to the rest.
(Workbook Lesson 198.2:8–10)

Forgiveness is the end of dreaming because it is awakening. Forgiveness is not the truth but it points to where the truth is. Once we have forgiven, we see that forgiveness wasn't necessary; we just thought it was. As difficult as this may sound, with the development of miracle-mindedness, we gradually begin to see all of life in a wholly different way and what seemed impossible becomes the only way to live.

Peace of mind occurs as we drop our concern with getting. Drop the need to be right, and concentrate on giving. Only then do we truly receive. Inner peace can be achieved only when we have forgiven. Forgiveness is the vehicle for changing our perception and letting go of our fear, condemnations, judgments, and grievances. There is nothing to forgive, unless we think there is. If we think there is something to forgive, then we have chosen to make an error real. We teach our brothers and sisters that they cannot hurt us by not making error real.

"There is nothing to hold on to.
Nothing!"

A Mercy

The quality of mercy is not strain'd,
It droppeth as the gentle rain from heaven
Upon the place beneath: it is twice blest;
It blesseth him that gives and him that takes:
'Tis mightiest in the mightiest: it becomes
The throned monarch better than his crown;
His sceptre shows the force of temporal power,
The attribute to awe and majesty,
Wherein doth sit the dread and fear of kings;
But mercy is above this sceptred sway;
It is enthroned in the hearts of kings,
It is an attribute to God himself;
And earthly power doth then show likest God's
When mercy seasons justice.

—William Shakespeare

5

The Freedom to Be at Peace

Frederick Buechner

To forgive somebody is to say one way or another, "You have done something unspeakable, and by all rights I should call it quits between us. Both my pride and my principles demand no less. However, although I make no guarantees that I will be able to forget what you've done, and though we may both carry the scars for life, I refuse to let it stand between us. I still want you for my friend."

To accept forgiveness means to admit that you've done something unspeakable that needs to be forgiven, and thus both parties must swallow the same thing: their pride.

This seems to explain what Jesus means when he says to God, "Forgive us our trespasses as we forgive those who trespass against us." Jesus is not saying that God's forgiveness is conditional upon our forgiving others. In the first place, forgiveness that's conditional isn't really forgiveness at all, just fair warning; and in the second place, our unforgivingness is among those things about us that we need to have God forgive us most. What Jesus apparently is saying is that the pride that keeps us from forgiving is the same pride that keeps us from accepting forgiveness, and will God please help us do something about it.

When somebody you've wronged forgives you, you're spared the dull and self-diminishing throb of a guilty conscience.

When you forgive somebody who has wronged you, you're spared the dismal corrosion of bitterness and wounded pride.

For both parties, forgiveness means the freedom again to be at peace inside their own skins and to be glad in each other's presence.

6

Giving and Receiving

Henri Nouwen

There are two sides to forgiveness: giving and receiving. Although at first sight giving seems to be harder, it often appears that we are not able to offer forgiveness to others because we have not been able fully to receive it. Only as people who have accepted forgiveness can we find the inner freedom to give it. Why is receiving forgiveness so difficult? It is very hard to say, "Without your forgiveness I am still bound to what happened between us. Only you can set me free." That requires not only a confession that we have hurt somebody but also the humility to acknowledge our dependency on others. Only when we can receive forgiveness can we give it.

7

I Want You Back: On Asking for Pardon

Eric Immel, SJ

There's a Spotify playlist out there called "Have a Great Day!" There are plenty of Spotify lists that miss the mark—"Weird Music," "Horror Movie Themes," and "Ambient Lounge" don't really do it for me. But when I walk into the office and get "Have a Great Day" rolling, the songs of Stevie, Aretha, Marvin, Hall and Oates all but guarantee that I will have a great day.

Inevitably, the playlist offers The Jackson 5's "I Want You Back" within the first ten tracks. The bright hollow body guitar and classic Motown bass line joined by little Michael's impressive lead vocal bring instant joy.

But on a recent morning, a great day seemed impossible. Not even the playlist could cure my abysmal mood. I wasn't willing to allow the joy of "I Want You Back" into my heart. Instead, I heard the lyrics: Give me one more chance to show you that I love you. Little Michael is asking for forgiveness. I needed to ask for some forgiveness, too.

◈◈◈

I get into these ruts sometimes.

A friend emailed months ago to say that he'd be in my current home—Chicago—over Memorial Day. And I didn't respond. Not entirely uncommon for me. He texted closer to the date, and again I offered no response. I had plans to visit my parents the same weekend, but I didn't tell him that. Then reasonably, if not frustratedly, he sent a second text, the content of which was a single punctuation mark: ?

And still I made no response.

Three messages from him, three moments of silence from me. He wanted to have dinner with his friend. He wanted to see me enough not to give up on getting my answer. But for some reason, I couldn't offer one.

Eventually, these things move from the simple act of managing my affairs into a category that I am truly terrified of—unfinished business.

This unfinished business lingers and lasts. It starts

with a momentary feeling of inadequacy and becomes another box to check off on a long list of things to do. Plan class for Tuesday: check. Follow up with co-worker about financial aid question: check. Set agenda for supervision: check.

But emailing or texting a friend back? It moves from list to list, unchecked and unacknowledged but never fully disappearing. Like a puddle close to evaporating, but not quite. The rain comes again and the puddle refills.

I finally called my friend on Saturday morning, the day after he arrived in Chicago. I wasn't even in the city. My bare feet brushed through the green grass in my parent's backyard hundreds of miles away, and I stared into the deep woods of my childhood. I was tired. I apologized. And, as a good friend does, he moved past his own desire to understand why it all happened the way it did in the first place. He simply offered forgiveness, pure and unmerited gift.

◈◈◈

There's another song out right now that I've been listening to on repeat. By no coincidence, it's called "Want You Back." In it, the lead singer names a deep and painful truth: I had a fear of forgiveness.

I'm not afraid to forgive. I practice offering it daily.

I'm also not afraid to be forgiven. When my friend and I finally talked, I felt deep relief and a sense of confirmation that our love for each other can survive my little ruts. Our love can survive my irrational ability to make a ten-second email or text response into a seemingly unbridgeable chasm between what I desire and what I actually do with that desire.

What I'm afraid of is asking for forgiveness. It means that I must acknowledge the inexcusable, inexplicable thing I've done. Maybe I don't feel like I deserve it. Maybe if I penned a pop song to send along, it would be easier.

◇◇◇

There's an email I've saved for over two years. It's from someone I once knew very well. In it, they describe a (no-longer) recent hardship they faced, and they asked me for my prayers. An email like that deserves a response. If this person knew the number of times I've actually offered my prayers, or the number of times I've thought of their email, or the number of times I've considered responding, they'd never doubt my love. But, for two years, the person who reached out hasn't known my side of the story, and now, all that's left is for me to respond with a few simple words.

Those words—please forgive me—could be the catalyst for a great day. A day when we together engage in the mystery that is forgiving. A day when that which has left me—a feeling of adequacy and worth and belovedness—will return. A day when all that is good between us comes back.

8

Failure and Forgiveness of Yourself

Robert J. Wicks

In "resiliency psychology and spirituality," my specialty for the past 30 years, one of the more recent areas of discussion and emphasis is referred to as "self-compassion." This may sound to some like narcissism or inordinate self-interest. However, a real understanding of it is far from this inaccurate understanding. Instead, healthy self-compassion has a proportionate impact on our ability to walk with others in their darkness. This is so because one of the greatest gifts we can share with others is a sense of our own peace and inner strength . . . but we can't share what we don't have!

An essential cornerstone of such appropriate self-compassion is the ability to forgive yourself when you fail. Involved spiritually committed persons fail a great deal. We probably don't like to talk about it, but it's true. As a group, we fail as much if not more than any other community concerned with helping others in need. This should not be surprising since with greater commitment there is a greater "opportunity" to miss at least some of the numerous goals we set for ourselves in life.

Yet, despite the fact that as persons of faith we court failure as a natural part of our idealism, many of us still punish ourselves mentally when we feel we have missed the mark—even if it was an almost impossible one. One of the most powerful ways of dealing with such a tendency is to embrace a proper sense of forgiveness about what we have failed to do or accomplish in our work with others or in facing our own shortcomings or sins.

To accomplish this we must first recognize and avoid false forms of forgiveness. "Pseudo-forgiveness" often parades itself as a form of true self-awareness. However, by its "fruits" it is possible to discern in ourselves and others whether or not the sense of forgiveness is properly oriented. There are surely numerous forms of pseudo-forgiveness. The one that particularly concerns us here is the one that forgets our humanity, inordinately focuses on the shame of our failures, and leads to an unproductive confession based only on ventilation of our shortcomings or sins.

Pseudo-forgiveness of self begins when in trying to be compassionate we forget that we can and *will* eventually fail. We forget that in trying to reach out to family, friends, co-workers, and even those in need who we do not know well, our own limits and needs must sometimes get in the way. When I was lecturing a group of surgical residents on resilience, self-care, and maintaining a healthy perspective, I cautioned them with the reality that during their tenure as surgeons, they would probably kill some people—not necessarily because of malpractice but because of "*mis*-practice." No one can operate on an "A" level 100 percent of the time no matter what their role. Parents do get tired and yell at their children even when they recognize (possibly later) that this was not the best thing to do. Others are sometimes short-tempered or condescending to the poor or chronically ill in their midst when they are not fully rested, have eliminated the space for personal "alone time" (periods of silence and solitude or being reflective even when in a group), or don't have enough balance in their schedule. At such times it is easy to forget that we are not perfect—only God is—and that with the right outlook we can learn from our failures rather than see them simply as proof that we shouldn't, or can't, be a compassionate presence to others in need.

When we as people trying to be spiritually faithful lose our perspective with regard to failure, we ignore the need for self-acceptance as a prelude to personal growth. In such cases, instead of forgiveness leading to an openness that will in turn translate into self-understanding, it leads to self-punishment or condemning others for their needs and situation. In such a case as this, we believe that we are seeking forgiveness by crucifying ourselves for our weakness. As we do this, the energy formerly reserved for knowledge gets destructively channeled off into changing the process of self-understanding into one of self-condemnation. Nothing positive is accomplished when this happens.

Ironically, this hurtful process of supposedly honest repentance *prevents* rather than enhances change and growth. The most obvious reason for this is that we are less apt to look at our behavior objectively if we are embarrassed or pained by reflection on it. Therefore, behavior that we wince at eventually turns into behavior that we wink at. If it causes us too much discomfort to look at something, psychologically we will avoid it through repression, suppression, denial, rationalization, and by general distortion of it.

So, how can we mine the fruits of personal failure when it occurs? Firstly, I think our attitude is key. It will determine if we can weather the storms of failure and a sense of loss when our goals are not achieved. In her memoir, *Dakota*, author Kathleen Norris wrote that she was called to reflect on this when she had come across a handwritten note by her grandmother inserted in an old family Bible. On it was written, "Keep me friendly to myself; keep me gentle in disappointment."

The second element is *clarity*. While we need to recognize the need to be kind so we don't cause narcissistic injury (hurt ourselves to the core of our personality), we also need to seek details about our failures, losses, and disappointments. If we are only gentle, we won't grow. If we only focus on our failures in a non-forgiving way, we will stunt our own growth. We need a balance of clarity in kindness in facing failure and forgiving ourselves for not being the person we wish to be in all situations.

The final element on the way to healthy self-forgiveness is to recognize that failure can teach us in much more powerful ways than success ever can. If we have the right balance of clarity and kindness, we will:

- Experience increased motivation and determination to face what we encounter as "darkness" or failure in ourselves
- Gain greater insight into who we are as persons because we will uncover our gifts, areas of vulnerability, and defenses
- Have less dependence on the recognition and approval of others
- Be in a better position to pick up more quickly the emotional cues that we are going to do something we will regret so we can stop ourselves
- Set the stage for the development of new skills and styles of interacting with others—especially in tough or chronically draining situations
- Appreciate, like St. Paul, that we must never shy away from seeing our failings or shortcomings clearly. However, also like Paul, we must ensure that in the same breath we must always also speak of God's grace so we don't fall into the trap of the "savior complex" and think we must never fail or have problems forgiving ourselves
- Know we can't ride the waves of life's stresses alone and expect we can always achieve our goals and gain the perspective on our own to know how and when to forgive ourselves. As Reinhold Niebuhr,

American ethicist, theologian, and commentator aptly notes, "Nothing we do, however virtuous, can be accomplished alone. . . ."

Finally, forgiveness of self also involves patience with ourselves so we can recognize that living a compassionate life involves tolerating discouragement and having the fortitude to continue in spite of the absence of immediate results. As Thomas Merton once said to a senior Trappist colleague who felt he was losing both his commitment and faith, "Brother, courage comes and goes . . . hold on for the next supply!"

In essence, when we truly understand the need for forgiveness of self when we fail, as we surely will at times, we will position ourselves to have a greater sense of inner peace that is independent of external success, comfort, and security. And, when we have such an attitude, think of what a gift that would be not only to ourselves but also to those we co-journey with as friend, family member, co-worker, or in a possibly professional role as helper or healer. Self-forgiveness is not a nicety. It is a necessity in today's anxious world.

9

Buddha's Lesson on Forgiveness

Quang Trí

The Buddha was sitting under a tree talking to his disciples when a man came and spit on his face. He wiped it off, and he asked the man, "What next? What do you want to say next?" The man was a little puzzled because he himself never expected that when you spit on somebody's face, he will ask, "What next?" He had no such experience in his past. He had insulted people and they had become angry and they had reacted. Or if they were cowards and weaklings, they had smiled, trying to bribe the man. But Buddha was like neither, he was not angry nor in any way offended, nor in any way cowardly. But just matter-of-factly he said, "What next?" There was no reaction on his part.

Buddha's disciples became angry, they reacted. His

closest disciple, Ananda, said, "This is too much, and we cannot tolerate it. He has to be punished for it. Otherwise everybody will start doing things like this."

Buddha said, "You keep silent. He has not offended me, but you are offending me. He is new, a stranger. He must have heard from people something about me, that this man is an atheist, a dangerous man who is throwing people off their track, a revolutionary, a corrupter. And he may have formed some idea, a notion of me. He has not spit on me, he has spit on his notion. He has spit on his idea of me because he does not know me at all, so how can he spit on me?

If you think on it deeply," Buddha said, "he has spit on his own mind. I am not part of it, and I can see that this poor man must have something else to say because this is a way of saying something. Spitting is a way of saying something. There are moments when you feel that language is impotent: in deep love, in intense anger, in hate, in prayer. There are intense moments when language is impotent. Then you have to do something. When you are angry, intensely angry, you hit the person, you spit on him, you are saying something. I can understand him. He must have something more to say, that's why I'm asking, 'What next?'"

The man was even more puzzled! And Buddha said to his disciples, "I am more offended by you because you know me, and you have lived for years with me, and still you react."

Puzzled, confused, the man returned home. He could not sleep the whole night. When you see a Buddha, it is difficult, impossible to sleep again the way you used to sleep before. Again and again he was haunted by the experience. He could not explain it to himself, what had happened. He was trembling all over and perspiring. He had never come across such a man; he shattered his whole mind and his whole pattern, his whole past.

The next morning he was back there. He threw himself at Buddha's feet. Buddha asked him again, "What next? This, too, is a way of saying something that cannot be said in language. When you come and touch my feet, you are saying something that cannot be said ordinarily, for which all words are a little narrow; it cannot be contained in them." Buddha said, "Look, Ananda, this man is again here, he is saying something. This man is a man of deep emotions."

The man looked at Buddha and said, "Forgive me for what I did yesterday."

Buddha said, "Forgive? But I am not the same man

to whom you did it. The Ganges goes on flowing, it is never the same Ganges again. Every man is a river. The man you spit upon is no longer here. I look just like him, but I am not the same; much has happened in these twenty-four hours! The river has flowed so much. So I cannot forgive you because I have no grudge against you.

And you also are new. I can see you are not the same man who came yesterday because that man was angry and he spit, whereas you are bowing at my feet, touching my feet. How can you be the same man? You are not the same man, so let us forget about it. Those two people, the man who spit and the man on whom he spit, both are no more. Come closer. Let us talk of something else."

Mercies

The most beautiful thing a man can do is to forgive wrong.

—Judaism

Forgive them for they do not know what they are doing.

—Christianity

My Lord, forgive my people for they do not know.

—Islam

10

The Comedy of Confession

Simcha Fisher

When I was younger, my family had to bribe me to go to confession once a year. I went literally dragging my feet and scowling like a demon.

I still do not like going to confession, but I sure do like having gone. Now when I exit the confessional, I have to hang on to the pews so as not to float away. Whatever kid I have dragged with me hears me say the same thing I always say: "You'll never get a better deal."

This week, I began collecting stories about confession from my Catholic social media friends, and I am not even sure why. I will start with one of my own: My husband and I both went to confession one afternoon. I got out first while he was still in line, and he asked me who was in there—the Nigerian nit-picker, the almost-deaf crank or maybe Father Distracto? I reared back in mock horror, rolled my eyes heavenward and whispered, "Um, it's Jesus."

If you cannot laugh at the ignominy of whispering your wretched little sins through a screen, then when will you laugh? When you don't have any breath left?

Many parents told me that when the priest raised his hand to absolve their kid on his first confession, the child mistook the gesture and gave father a triumphant high five: Absolvo! Down low—he's too slow! In peace you go.

Sometimes the joke is more subtle. One woman said that as an adult convert she had a terrible time working herself up to go to confession for the first time. When she finally got there, she was astonished to find there was no priest. No sign, no message, no nothing. She took it as a sign that she was on the right track. If getting absolution were easy, it probably would not be worth doing.

Sometimes there is no joke at all, just the tenderness of Christ. Another woman, a revert, said: "The first confession I made after being away for six years, the priest kindly and patiently listened to me sob out my sins. When I could not go on because I was crying so hard, he gently began to counsel me. My penance was the search for Christ's love within me. A few days later, I found out I was pregnant with my first child—out of wedlock with my boyfriend whom I then married, and we now have five kids."

Many penitents have stories of slinking into the box sunk deep in gloom and remorse, only to encounter a jolly priest who thinks everything is fixable, chucks you under the chin, offers you a Tootsie Roll with your absolution, and reminds you that you can maybe get over yourself.

More than one penitent somehow pocket-dialed an acquaintance and left a long, emotional, very personal voicemail from the box. And we have all run into priests and penitents alike who are just plain loud, leaving the reluctant audience outside to cough, shuffle their feet, jingle their car keys and conclude that they, too, are bound by the seal of confession, no matter how unwillingly they heard what they heard.

There are priests who are hard of hearing or just plain confused and give draconian penances based on sins the penitent never confessed or who holler out, "You did what!" for all the congregation to hear.

It is strangely comforting to know how universal these stories are. Catholics all over the world suffer the same tragicomedies as they take their chances in the confessional.

There are priests who fold their aching bodies into the box, week after week; priests who put aside their own weariness and malaise to offer hope, encouragement, and forgiveness, week after week. Priests who draw contrition out of the defiant, resolve out of the reluctant, and peace out of the inconsolable. There are priests who walk in willingly, knowing they are expected to be therapist, referee, mind-reader, and punching bag all in one.

And then there are priests who withhold absolution because they do not like the penitent's tone. There are priests who think the penitent cannot possibly be sorry because she keeps confessing the same thing every week. Priests who lash out, grumble, harangue, or even mock. There are priests who meet the wounded and, in the name of Christ, add to their wounds. There are priests, in short, who let their human weakness, foolishness, prejudice, and personal sin overcome their training and their duty and who run the risk of chasing a sinner away from Christ for good—the very opposite of what he is there to do.

Strange to say, I found this kind of story comforting, too, because most of the people who told these stories did come back. Years later, they were still angry or wounded. Some complained to the bishop. Some left the church for years. But eventually, they did come back, back to the church, back to the sacraments.

Why? Because, as I snarkily reminded my husband, it is Jesus in there.

Sometimes that is obvious. Sometimes we hear exactly what we needed to hear and find peace and healing where none seemed possible. But sometimes we must rely on our faith to remember that the sacrament's power comes not from the man but through him, from God.

It is Jesus in there. If you cannot whisper out your sins through the grill to him while you still have breath, then when? If you will not meet him in the person of the priest, then to whom will you go? It does not matter whose name is posted outside the confessional. It is Jesus in there, and that is why it is always worth coming back.

11

Beyond Ideas

Pierre Eau Claire

(*"Out beyond ideas of wrongdoing and rightdoing,*

there is a field. I'll meet you there."—Rumi)

Beyond philosophy,
beyond psychology,
beyond ethics,
there is a realm of existence
where we simply are together
without judgment or hostility.

I search for that field now
within my heart.
It's there that we shall meet
and experience the grace of peace.

Part Two

FORGIVING OTHERS

Seventy Times Seven

Matthew 18:21

Then Peter came to him and said, “Lord, how often shall my brother sin against me, and I forgive him? Up to seven times?”

Jesus said to him, “I do not say to you, up to seven times, but up to seventy times seven.”

12

a total stranger one black day

e. e. cummings

a total stranger one black day
knocked living the hell out of me—

who found forgiveness hard because
my(as it happened)self he was

—but now that fiend and i are such
immortal friends the other's each

13

They Do Not Know What They Are Doing

James Martin, SJ

As they led him away, they seized a man, Simon of Cyrene, who was coming from the country, and they laid the cross on him, and made him carry it behind Jesus. A great number of the people followed him, and among them were women who were beating their breasts and wailing for him. But Jesus turned to them and said, "Daughters of Jerusalem, do not weep for me, but weep for yourselves and for your children. For the days are surely coming when they will say, 'Blessed are the barren, and the wombs that never bore, and the breasts that never nursed.' Then they will begin to say to the mountains, 'Fall on us'; and to the hills, 'Cover us.' For if they do this when the wood is green, what will happen when it is dry?"

Two others also, who were criminals, were led away to be put to death with him. When they came to the place that is called The Skull, they crucified Jesus there with the criminals, one on his right and one on his left. Then Jesus said, "Father, forgive them; for they do not know what they are doing." And they cast lots to divide his clothing. And the people stood by, watching; but the leaders scoffed at him, saying, "He saved others; let him save himself if he is the Messiah of God, his chosen one!" The soldiers also mocked him, coming up and offering him sour wine and saying, "If you are the King of the Jews, save yourself!"

—LUKE 23:26–37

◈◈◈

In our sometimes dark world we are often given moments of light that not only illumine our way, but remind us that God is with us.

One kind of these moments happens frequently, and you've probably heard about it, read about it, or even encountered it yourself. I'm speaking about moments of radical forgiveness: those amazing stories, which you've seen in newspapers, on television, or online, of men and women forgiving people responsible for horrific crimes committed against them or, more typically, against members of their families.

A Jesuit friend, for example, once told me a moving story about his family. One night, his father was awakened from a deep sleep and told that his sixteen-year-old son had been killed in a car accident while being driven by a friend named Kenny, who was drunk at the time. At the trial, the father pleaded with the judge to give Kenny the minimum sentence possible, because Kenny never wanted to kill his friend.

Afterward, my Jesuit friend asked his father how he could possibly do that. His father said, "I just did what I thought was right." He also said that he saw Kenny as more than just that one terrible act. Today, my friend's father still keeps in touch with Kenny, who now has his own children. For his part, Kenny has written faithfully for the last twenty years to the father of the boy whose death he caused.

And recently *America* magazine, where I work as an editor, published the remarkable story of a woman named Jeanne—an attorney, as it happens—who forgave the man who killed her sister, her sister's husband, and their unborn child. The killer was remorseless and had never admitted his guilt.

Now here is a story of not an accidental death, but an intentional one, and—let me repeat—there was no remorse. I repeat that because many people believe you can't forgive someone who isn't sorry.

But Jeanne was able to forgive her sister's murderer. She said that at the time the phrase "You take away the sins of the world," which Catholics recite during the Mass, deeply moved her. Jeanne said she wasn't sure if she'd ever fully understand what those words mean, but they surely don't mean that we should take the sin a person commits and freeze it; that no matter what the person does, even if he or she repents, we should punish the person for it forever. It's similar to what Sister Helen Prejean, CSJ, the author of *Dead Man Walking*, often says about inmates on death row: "People are more than the worst thing they've ever done in their lives."

Years later, Jeanne realized that she had never told her sister's murderer that she had forgiven him. So she wrote him a letter and did so.

In response, Jeanne received a letter of confession and remorse. He wrote, "You're right, I am guilty of killing your sister . . . and her husband. . . . I also want to take this opportunity to express my deepest condolences and apologize to you."

Forgiveness had freed him to be honest and remorseful.

I'm sure you've heard stories like this. I'm sure you've also seen occasions of the more common situation, where victims are given the opportunity in the courtroom to respond to the criminals, and they do *not* forgive. I'm sure you've seen videos of family members screaming at criminals: "I want you to suffer like I am!" "I hope you rot in jail!" "I hope you fry in the electric chair!" "I hope you go to hell!" It's understandable. Anyone who is the victim of a crime or the relative or friend of a victim—particularly of a violent crime—should be forgiven for being angry.

I would probably feel the same way. It's human.

But the reason we respond so powerfully to those other situations, where radical forgiveness is offered, is that they're divine. That's why they touch us. Those moments speak to the deepest part of ourselves, which instinctively recognizes the divine. We see these moments as beautiful, because this is how God wants us to live. It's a kind of call.

Now you may say, "Those are nice words, Father, but you don't live in the real world. What do you know about that?"

Let me assure you, even in religious orders and in the priesthood one can find anger, bitterness, and ill will. But it's easy to see where people get that idea. I'm sometimes susceptible to that kind of romanticism myself. Once I said to a Benedictine monk, "Well,

I'm sure it's easier in a monastery than it is in a Jesuit community."

He just laughed and told me a funny story. One elderly monk in his community used to show his displeasure with other monks in a highly creative way. As you may know, most monastic communities chant the psalms several times a day together in chapel. Well, if this elderly monk was angry at someone, every time the word "enemy" came up in a psalm, as in "Deliver me from my enemies," he would look up from his prayer book and glare at the monk he was angry with.

On a more personal note, I once lived in a community with a Jesuit who more or less refused to talk to me for ten years. He despised me and made that clear in almost every interaction we had—whether alone or in a group. At one point, I asked him if I had done anything to offend him, and he refused to answer. I never figured out what prompted his hatred, and he never changed his attitude. In desperation, I asked an elderly Jesuit priest, renowned for his holiness, for advice.

The only thing to do, he told me, is to forgive.

Now, you might be thinking of a situation in your own life and say, "I can never forgive. It's impossible." Then look at what Jesus does from the cross. If anyone had the right not to forgive, it was Jesus. If anyone had the right to lash out in anger, it was Jesus. If anyone had the right to feel unjustly persecuted, it was Jesus. Yet even though the Roman soldiers do not express remorse in front of him, Jesus not only forgives them; he prays for them. Notice that. Jesus says, "Father, forgive them." He's praying for them.

Now consider that line, "They do not know what they are doing." That particular phrase helped me a great deal with the Jesuit who wouldn't speak to me. He didn't seem to know what he was doing. Indeed, people who sin sometimes don't seem to be thinking clearly. This insight may help you on your road to forgiveness. It's the same impulse that allows you to easily forgive a mentally ill person for doing something that seems thoughtless, rude, or even cruel.

Jesus does the same thing. Jesus always *sees*. And he sees beyond what people around him see. He sees people for who they really are. Forgiveness is a gift you give the other person and yourself. Jesus knows this. And he not only tells us this several times in the Gospels, but he shows us this. He is teaching us even from the cross.

14

The Long Road to Forgiveness

Kim Phuc

On June 8, 1972, I ran out from Cao Dai temple in my village, Trang Bang, South Vietnam. I saw an airplane getting lower and then four bombs falling down. I saw fire everywhere around me. Then I saw the fire over my body, especially on my left arm. My clothes had been burned off by fire.

I was nine years old but I still remember my thoughts at that moment: I would be ugly and people would treat me in a different way. My picture was taken in that moment on Road I from Saigon to Phnom Penh. After a soldier gave me some drink and poured water over my body, I lost my consciousness.

Several days after, I realized that I was in the hospital, where I spent fourteen months and had seventeen operations. It was a very difficult time for me when I went home from the hospital. Our house was destroyed, we lost everything, and we just survived day by day.

Although I suffered from pain, itching, and headaches all the time, the long hospital stay made me dream to become a doctor. But my studies were cut short by the local government. They wanted me as a symbol of the state. I could not go to school any more.

The anger inside me was like a hatred as high as a mountain. I hated my life. I hated all people who were normal because I was not normal. I really wanted to die many times.

I spent my daytime in the library to read a lot of religious books to find a purpose for my life. One of the books that I read was the Holy Bible. On Christmas 1982, I accepted Jesus Christ as my personal savior. It was an amazing turning point in my life. God helped me to learn to forgive—the most difficult of all lessons. It didn't happen in a day and it wasn't easy. But I finally got it.

Forgiveness made me free from hatred. I still have many scars on my body and severe pain most days, but my heart is cleansed.

Napalm is very powerful but faith, forgiveness, and love are much more powerful. We would not have war at all if everyone could learn how to live with true love, hope, and forgiveness. If that little girl in the picture can do it, ask yourself: Can you?

A Mercy

Some time ago, Eufrasio, an elder of an Aymara clan in the Altiplano of Peru, came to his parish priest and asked if he might use his house for a meeting. The priest assured him that it would be fine. Eufrasio thanked him and said, "We want you to be there as well."

When the day arrived, quite a number of Aymara folks came for the meeting. It seems there had been an incident that had angered people and resulted in many hurt feelings in the group. The elder stood before the group and asked one man to stand and tell his side of the story, which he did. He then asked someone of the opposite opinion to tell his version. After each had spoken, Eufrasio suggested a solution to the problem—and all agreed. He then asked each person present to give a sign of peace to everyone else in the room. When this was done he said, "Now this will never be mentioned again." All left quietly in peace.

Eufrasio then turned to the priest, thanked him for allowing them to use his house, and he too left.

"Now I have truly witnessed the sacrament of reconciliation," said the priest.

—Helen Phillips, MM

15

Forgiveness Is the Only Thing That Is New in the World

Ron Rolheiser

When one reads Helen Prejean's *Dead Man Walking*, what is often lost in the sheer power of the story is what she recounts at the very end of the book and intends precisely as the real ending to the story.

The book ends with the story of Lloyd LeBlanc, the father of the boy who was murdered, and his struggle to forgive his son's killer.

After the execution of the man who killed his son, Prejean describes how she would occasionally meet Lloyd LeBlanc at a chapel which holds perpetual adoration. Kneeling with him, in the middle of the night in a silent chapel, they would say the rosary together. Prejean describes how, at a point, he shared with her his struggle to forgive his son's killer.

When he arrived with the sheriff's deputies in the

deserted field to identify his son's body, he had knelt down beside the body and prayed the Our Father. When he came to the words: "Forgive us our trespasses as we forgive those who trespass against us," he had not stopped praying or made any mental reservations. Instead he added the words: "Whoever did this, I forgive them."

There, beside his dead son's mutilated body, he had forgiven the man who had done that to his son.

This is truly extraordinary. To be kneeling beside the dead body of your own child and be able to say: "Whoever did this, I forgive them," requires a big faith and even a bigger heart.

But Lloyd LeBlanc admits that it has not been easy to sustain that forgiveness. Bitterness continues to well up inside of him, especially on days like his son's birthday and other days when the memory of his son and the senselessness of his death simply overwhelm him. He confesses that the struggle is constant and the forgiveness he once gave must be given over and over again.

But obviously forgiveness is winning out because, among other things, he was even able to go and visit the mother of his son's killer, when she herself lay dying, and offer her comfort.

I bring up the example of Lloyd LeBlanc because forgiveness is the one thing that we do not do well. Lack of forgiveness is our Achilles' heel. As much as we like to protest—and for all of our moral, intellectual and technological achievements, our political correctness and our espoused sensitivities—our world, our communities, our churches, our families and our personal lives are shot full of hatred, anger, resentments, grudges, and long-remembered wounds.

Everywhere we turn, somebody is nursing a grudge; somebody has a history which justifies an anger; and somebody is protesting that, in his or her case, the call to forgiveness does not apply. All of which is an infallible sign that our hearts are not near the size of our faith.

We rationalize this non-forgiveness in every kind of way: If I am more crass, I simply say: "I don't forget, I get even."

However, if I am more sophisticated, or at least pretend to be, I rationalize the refusal to forgive by saying: "I have a fierce desire for justice and there can be no forgiveness until there is justice." "I have been victimized and therefore am above the demand for forgiveness—at least right now, at least as it pertains to this particular thing, or at least as it pertains to this particular person or group."

"Nobody knows my pain and pain such as mine justifies my bitterness and anger." "The challenge to forgive is easily spoken by those in power and those who have done the wrong—I wonder how they would feel if they were on the other end!"

In each of these cases, unspoken but present, is the subordinate clause—"and thus I have the right to hate!" In each case too, unspoken but present, there is a bracketing of a key subordinate clause in the Lord's Prayer, "as we forgive those who trespass against us."

To err is human, to forgive is divine. Forgiveness is not something we human beings can do all on our own. Forgiveness is a non-human power that God gives to the world in the resurrection of Jesus.

And it is here that all of us can learn a lesson, maybe the most important one of our lives, from Lloyd LeBlanc. He could have rationalized a perpetual bitterness under any of the slogans quoted above, but he didn't. He forgave, immediately and without qualification, the killer of his son.

Prejean shares with us that Lloyd LeBlanc sustains his faith and his forgiveness in a rather simple, straightforward way: He goes to churches, kneels in adoration and prays the rosary, especially using the sorrowful mysteries, asking God to give him a strength that he knows he does not have. And he does this over and over and over again.

Forgiveness is the only thing that is new in the world, the one sure sign that there is a God. The example of Lloyd LeBlanc is an icon of that.

16

Sour Memories

Joyce Rupp

My teacher has come to live next door,
the stranger I least choose to be here
where we each come for our own retreat.
A tall, aging, ordained man swishes
past my window in his long, black cassock,
seemingly sure of himself
with his obsolete, unsettling beliefs.

I hear irritating noise in the next room
where the man knows nothing of silence—
maybe of the tongue, but not of the body.
The door clangs when he leaves his room;
at 5:00 a.m. he runs water at full blast
and forcefully slams the closet doors
like an old elephant without balance.
With each noisy intrusion
sour memories rise to the surface in me.

The Way of Forgiveness

But it's the black robe, the white collar
announcing a presumed entitlement
that stirs up the odor of my indignation.
It's the trouncing voice of hierarchy,
in varied forms of arrogant posture,
that revisits me like musty onions
left to rot in the corner of a cupboard.

What to do but wonder—why now,
why here, why this—only to surmise
it is one more graced opportunity
to rid my soul of fermented antipathy,
to dismiss the contempt that robs me
of a kinder, compassionate spirit.

One more time I lean into the past
and release the mildewed memories;
one more time I allow forgiveness
to cleanse another bit of fetid residue.

17

"So, I Opted to Go for It"

Lynn F. Monahan

Two years after gaining independence as a new nation in 2011, South Sudan once again slipped into civil war, the third time in almost fifty years. This time the conflict is between the country's two largest ethnic groups, the Dinka led by President Salva Kiir and the Nuer led by former Vice President Riek Machar. More than 1.2 million people have fled South Sudan to escape the fighting. Among them is Ocan Robert Venderiko, 31, a clan leader of the Acholi tribe. A Catholic, like the majority of the Acholi, Robert strives to be a peacebuilder in his divided community from the town of Pajok who are now in the Palabek Refugee Settlement in Uganda. He spoke with Lynn F. Monahan, editor-in-chief of Maryknoll *magazine, there in January.*

"Everybody is here. The ex-combatants from both sides are here. And then you have the civil population. . . . We don't know when the war will end, and so if we allow the rift to continue, by the time the war ends, we'll be having a lot of wounds in the heart that cannot be healed. . . . 'Oh, you're the one who did this. It was you who made my brother to be killed. It was you who looted.' So, we need to be closing some of these small, small chapters immediately as they come out.

"This politic broke the Acholi as a tribe in two. So, you are either for the government or you are treated as a rebel supporter. . . . Our community is strategic. It is close to the border. There's water flowing. The community is an agricultural community; there's a lot of food. And then there's some mountains. So (the rebels) chose our area to be their base. . . . There are times when the government comes and attacks them. . . . The community sort of changed hands between rebels and the government forces.

"I personally found myself knocking heads with the rebels and with the government until at one point the rebels came and arrested me with other leaders who worked with me in South Sudan. We were detained for three days, thrown down a big hole. I personally was given 100 lashes with some of the leaders. . . . Then they released us.

"The community was on a knife edge and all depended on me. If I were to go with revenge and hatred, that would mean the community would take that direction immediately. So, I opted to go for forgiveness.

"For example, when we came in April, some of the rebels left and fled with us. Among them was one who executed the order of this commander who gave me the 100 lashes. . . . The police told him, 'With this we cannot let you stay in the reception with the rest of the community because it will be risky. Some people will know you are on the rebel side, and some ex-combatants from the government side who are here will not see you well, so we will take you to the house of the refugee leader.'

"He was brought to my house, the one who lashed me. . . . So, I accommodated him, gave him water; he bathed, he ate, and the next morning we took breakfast. . . . It was not easy for my wife anyway. But I calmed her down and I explained to her. At last, when he was leaving in the morning, he told me, 'When you offend an individual and you don't reconcile, it's the worst offense.' I told him, 'This is life. You and I have to lead the process of forgiveness again.' So, he's here in the settlement and we are living with him. . . . It's not an easy step but you have to do it so you have the courage and the energy to speak to people and challenge them to reconcile and forgive each other."

18

Antoinette Bosco—Model of Forgiveness

Michael Leach

Love your enemies and pray for those who hurt you, that you may be children of your loving Father in heaven. God's sun shines on the good and the bad, and his rain falls on the righteous and the unrighteous.

—Matthew 5:44–45

Amazon.com lists 160,510 books on the topic of forgiveness. That's 31,629 more than on sexuality. What does that tell us about the human heart and what it hungers for most?

As an editor and publisher, I ask authors to write on topics that interest me deeply. Over the years I've asked more authors to write on the topic of forgiveness than any other. That's because I want to get it right in my own life. Nothing is more important. Who of us doesn't desire the freedom that comes when we let go of resentments that sear our souls, or the joy that makes our hearts soar when we ourselves experience forgiveness?

The two best books on forgiveness I've ever published are both by Antoinette (Toni) Bosco. Toni is a woman who knows what she's talking about. She lost one son to suicide and another son and his wife to the hands of a coldblooded killer. Can you imagine how she felt toward God, toward herself, and toward the murderer of her child? Toni's life since has been a dramatic journey to radical forgiveness and inner peace.

When her youngest son Peter, the joy of her life, killed himself at twenty-seven, Toni, a single mother, did not have much time to grieve. She had to help her other six children who adored Peter get through their grief. Peter had first suffered a nervous breakdown when he was seventeen. With the help of family and professionals, he slowly recovered and went on to write three books, one of them on World War I and another on the War of 1812. Peter hated war and when the Gulf War started he felt he could no longer live in this kind of world. His suicide note said, "Be happy for your son. . . . My pain is gone."

Toni was still mourning Peter's death when two years later the phone rang in the middle of the night. It was a Montana sheriff, two thousand miles away from the Bosco home in Connecticut.

"Are you Antoinette Bosco?" he asked.

"Yes," she answered.

"Do you have a son, John Bosco?"

"What's wrong? What happened?"

"I'm sorry to have to tell you this but we have a crime scene here. He and his wife are dead."

Toni couldn't speak.

When she climbed up the stairs of their Montana home and entered the blood-soaked bedroom, Toni wanted to kill the killer with her bare hands. She wanted him dead.

She would break into a sweat every time she saw in her mind's eye the eighteen-year-old with the unlikely name of Shadow Clark crawling through the basement window into her children's home, sneaking up the stairs to the bedroom where they slept, and then, afraid they would awaken, shoot them to death with a semi-automatic gun.

"In time, in spite of my grieving, which will always be a permanent part of my life, I knew I had to reclaim my soul, but how? I had to struggle long and hard with

whether forgiveness made sense, whether it was even possible. My children helped me as we struggled together with this horror. We had always been opposed to the death penalty, and began to grasp again that the state is no more justified in taking a life than an individual. Our healing began when we wrote to the judge, asking that Shadow Clark not be executed. I could say he must be punished for life, but I could not say, kill this killer.

"I learned to see that the minute we say 'no' to forgiveness we are gouging Christ out of our life, and from that resulting emptiness of soul we have nothing left to give to anybody else.

"To forgive is just what the word itself says—to offer a gift before it's been earned or even deserved. It doesn't mean giving in, it means letting go. If we don't forgive we stay emotionally handcuffed to the person—or the nation—that hurt us. And if we're handcuffed, we are not free, never at peace, never able to do God's work. Forgiveness is a boomerang—the gift we send out is what we're going to get back. This is how God treats us. When we forgive, we act as God does."

Toni realized it was foolishness to think that her pain would end by making someone else feel pain. She knew that revenge, too, was a boomerang. Her whole life as a Catholic taught her to rely on the teachings of Jesus to get through suffering. She knew that Jesus' entire life was about forgiveness. "Now again he was helping me take the actions that would bring healing. Each step in my life was clearly marked with directions—*Forgive!* Forgive your troubled Peter, forgive the young killer of your John and Nancy, forgive yourself."

Without asking for it, Toni soon became a national advocate against capital punishment. She has been invited to speak against the death penalty at high schools and colleges, in parishes and in prisons. The U.S. Conference of Catholic Bishops asked her to speak to them on forgiveness. The U.S. Senate asked her to submit testimony at a special hearing on the death penalty.

"When we are crushed like grapes," wrote Henri Nouwen, "we cannot think of the wine we will become."

Toni Bosco is vintage spirituality.

She speaks to *us* in *Radical Forgiveness:*

"Few people, thank God, have to deal with forgiving someone who murdered a loved one, or a beloved child who is defeated in life and ends his or her pain by killing themselves. But all of us must deal on a regular basis with thoughts about people we feel have hurt us, abandoned

us, spoken badly about us, hurt our feelings, damaged our reputations, manipulated, provoked, or just plain annoyed us. They can be parents, relatives, friends, bosses, employees, or strangers.

"But it is not these people we need to forgive so much as our thoughts about them, the angry, unforgiving thoughts that gnaw at our consciousness, burn us, haunt us, won't let us go, because we can't let them go. I have learned that radical forgiveness, asked for and given, seventy times seven times is the only way out of that prison."

A prize-winning journalist, Toni has written more than 200 magazine articles, thousands of newspaper stories, and ten books, but was awarded the Christopher Award, the Catholic Press Award, and the Pax Christi Award for two of her books on forgiveness: *The Pummeled Heart* and *Choosing Mercy: A Mother of Murder Victims Pleads to End the Death Penalty.* Yes, there are 160,510 books on forgiveness and many of them are extraordinary but Toni Bosco, you can be sure, knows what she is talking about. Her example enables the rest of us to deal with the "little murders"—gossip, backstabbing, envy, resentment—that torture each of us.

Many Catholics feel resentment toward God or the church. No one can blame them. But it may help for all of us to know that Catholicism, spiritually understood, was a source of healing for Toni Bosco, "a woman who has suffered greatly" (Mark 5:26) and who is one of the most together people you could ever know. "Buoyed by the grace of God," she says, "I found my answer. It is not to want more death. It is to celebrate *life*" (John 10:10).

Mercies

And now here is my secret, a very simple secret: It is only with the heart that one can see rightly; what is essential is invisible to the eye.

—The Little Prince

Dumbledore says people find it far easier to forgive others for being wrong than being right.

—Harry Potter and the Half-Blood Prince

I wondered if that was how forgiveness budded; not with the fanfare of epiphany, but with pain gathering its things, packing up, and slipping away unannounced in the middle of the night.

—The Kite Runner

19

Love Your Enemies! What Does It Mean? Can It Be Done?

David Steindl-Rast, OSB

As I walked out the door toward the gate that would lead to my freedom, I knew if I didn't leave my bitterness and hatred behind, I'd still be in prison.

—Nelson Mandela

To love our enemies does not mean that we suddenly become their friends. If it is our enemies we are to love, they must remain enemies. Unless you have enemies, you cannot love them. And if you have no enemies, I wonder if you have any friends. The moment you choose your friends, their enemies become your own enemies. By having convictions, we make ourselves the enemies of those who oppose these convictions. But let's be sure we agree on what we mean by terms like Friend, Enemy, Hatred, or Love.

The mutual intimacy we share with our best friends is one of the greatest gifts of life, but it is not always given when we call someone a friend. Friendship need not even be mutual. How about organizations like Friends of Our Local Library? Friends of Elephants and of other endangered species? Friendship allows for many degrees of closeness and takes many different forms. What it always implies is active support of those whom we befriend, engagement to help them reach their goals.

With enemies it is the exact opposite. After all, the very word "enemy" comes from the Latin "inimicus," and means simply "not a friend." Of course, not everyone who is not a friend is therefore an enemy. Enemies are opponents—not opponents for play, as in sports or games, but in mutual opposition with us in matters of deep concern. Their goals are opposed to our own highest aspirations. Thus, out of conviction we must actively try to prevent them from reaching their goals. We can do this lovingly, or not—and thus we find ourselves head-on confronted with the possibility to love of enemies.

Love makes us first of all think of romantic attraction, affection, and desire—a whirlwind of emotions, yes, but that is only one of countless forms in which we experience love. In so many different contexts do we speak of love that one may actually wonder what they have in common, if anything: Love between teacher and pupil, love of parents for children, of children for parents; love of your dog or your cats, your country, your grandparents. Again, how different our love for a grandmother is from that for a grandfather and both of them from love for a pet geranium among our potted plants, let alone love for a sweetheart. Is there a common denominator for all these varieties of love? Yes, indeed, there is.

To love our enemies may be our only way out.

Love in every one of its forms is a lived "yes" to belonging. I call it a "lived yes," because the very way loving people live and act says loudly and clearly: "Yes, I affirm and respect you and I wish you well. As members of the cosmic family we belong together, and this belonging goes far deeper than anything that can ever divide us." In an upside-down way, a "Yes" to belonging is even present in hatred. While love says this yes joyfully and with fondness, hatred says it grudgingly with animosity, gall. Still, even one who hates acknowledges mutual belonging. Have there not been moments in your life when you couldn't say whether you loved or hated someone close to your heart? This shows that hatred is not the opposite of love. The opposite of love (and of hatred) is indifference.

How, then, can we go about loving our enemies?

• Show your enemies the genuine respect that every human being deserves. Learn to think of them with compassion.

• In cultivating compassion, it may help to visualize your enemies as the children they once were (and somehow remain).

• Do not dispense compassion from above, but meet your enemies in your imagination always at eye-level.

• Make every effort to come to know and understand them better—their hopes, their fears, concerns, and aspirations.

• Search for common goals, spell them out, and try to explore together ways of reaching these goals.

• Don't cling to your own convictions. Examine them in light of your enemies' convictions with all the sincerity you can muster.

• Invite your enemies to focus on issues. While focusing on the issues at hand, suspend your convictions.

• Do not judge persons, but look closely at the

effect of their actions. Are they building up or endangering the common good?

• Take a sober look at your enemies' goals and evaluate them with fairness. If necessary, block them decisively.

• In order to counteract your enemies effectively on a given issue, join the greatest possible variety of like-minded people.

• Wherever possible, show your enemies kindness. Do them as much good as you can. At least, sincerely wish them well.

• For the rest, entrust yourself and your enemies to the great Mystery of life that has assigned us such different—and often opposing—roles, and that will see us through if we play or part with love.

Loving our enemies is an ideal for human beings of any spiritual tradition. Mahatma Gandhi practiced it no less inspiringly than St. Francis. But it calls to mind the saying of Jesus: "You have heard that it was said, 'You shall love your neighbor and hate your enemy.' But I say to you, Love your enemies and pray for those who persecute you" (Mt. 3:43). And this, in turn, calls to mind what G. K. Chesterton said: "The Christian ideal has not been tried and found wanting. It has been found difficult; and left untried."—

Difficult, yes, but eminently worth trying, especially in our world torn by enmity. In the mess we are in, we don't have much to lose by trying anything. Who knows? To love our enemies may be our only way out.

20

Practicing the Fine Art of Forgiveness

Victor Parachin

As we grow in wisdom, we pardon more freely
—Anne-Louise Germaine De Stael

This small footnote in history offers a large lesson in practicing the fine art of forgiveness. In 1922, Walter Rathenau, Germany's Jewish foreign minister, was assassinated by three German right-wing extremists. The men who committed this murder were motivated by political ideology and anti-Semitism. When the police captured them, two of them ended their lives by suicide. Only one of them survived to face trial, a man named Ernst Werner Techow.

Three days after the assassination, Mathilde Rathenau, the victim's mother, wrote to Techow's mother saying:

> In grief unspeakable, I give you my hand . . . Say to your son that, in the name and spirit of him he has murdered, I forgive, even as God may forgive, if before an earthly judge your son makes a full and frank confession of his guilt . . . and before a heavenly judge repents. Had he known my son, the noblest man earth bore, he would have rather turned the weapon on himself. May these words give peace to your soul.

Her words were read in open court and the public wondered if they would have any effect on the young assassin. Two decades later Techow would tell a Rathenau relative that the letter was his "most precious possession . . . it opened a new world to me." In prison he began to study seriously Jewish history and culture. He mastered Hebrew, becoming an erudite scholar of Judaism. In addition, Techow became highly sensitized to issues of anti-Semitism.

Sentenced to fifteen years, Techow was released from prison for good behavior after five years. In 1940, when France surrendered to Nazi Germany, Techow spotted an opportunity to repay Mathilde Rathenau's gracious act of forgiveness. He smuggled himself into Marseilles, where he began helping Jews to escape Nazi-dominated France. Techow was able to buy—or have forged—exit visas and permits allowing Jews to flee France for the safety of Spain. Always on the lookout for Jews he could help, Techow once asked a friend, "Do you know any Jews I could help to get out of here?" When the friend said he knew many, but that they had no money, Techow said: "Don't let that bother you. To be sure, those who are rich will have to pay a reasonable fee. But for every rich man I sponsor there are three penniless I help to escape for nothing."

In all, Techow helped over seven hundred Jews escape to Spain. No Jew who came to him was turned away. He provided the same service to those who were penniless and desperate as he did to those who could cover his expenses. Techow explained that his transformation and compassion toward Jewish people was set in motion by Mathilde Rathenau's letter: "Just as Frau Rathenau conquered herself when she wrote that letter of pardon, I have tried to master myself. I only wished I would get an opportunity to right the wrong I've done."

Forgiveness is a major theme in Judaism, Christianity, and Islam. It is also a highly regarded virtue in Eastern religious philosophy, and those spiritual teachers offer a variety of practices to develop a spirit of forgiveness. Eastern thinking understands that forgiveness is compassion in action. It has the power to uplift and transform our lives, and, sometimes, the lives of those whom we forgive. Forgiveness helps shed pain, bitterness, anger, and even hatred. Here is a six-step forgiveness meditation to practice when you are feeling wounded by someone else's words or deeds.

1. *Relaxation:* Use a quiet place where you won't be disturbed or distracted. Light a candle to symbolize the eternal light of divine love, compassion, and forgiveness. Sit comfortably on a cushion or a chair. Begin to relax your mind, spirit, emotions. Many find relaxation comes more easily when they focus on their breath. Simply breathe in and out, slowly and intentionally. Do this to a count of forty. Then meditate on the deity of your choice, asking for help in forgiving the person who hurt you.

2. *Recall* the person who hurt you and the words or actions that offended you. Without vilifying the person, simply focus on how you are feeling: angry, hurt, betrayed, bitter, furious, etc.

3. *Reframe* your experience by thinking of the other person. Understand that this person, like yourself, is

changing every moment. Put yourself in his or her shoes. Try to see that they believed that their words or actions would give them pleasure or help them avoid suffering. Such motivations are often no different from our own.

4. *Respond* with forgiveness. Using the name of the person, say out loud: "I forgive you."

5. *Recognize* that you have made an intentional effort to forgive. Thank your deity or higher power for helping you with this effort.

6. *Repeat* this meditation as often as necessary and until you feel your forgiveness is complete. It often takes a series of forgiveness meditations to reach wholeness and peace.

21

Meanest

Pierre Eau Claire

Though but six years on this planet,
though a member of a caring family,
though the youngest of four siblings,
she told her mother in a loud voice:
"You are the meanest mother in the whole world."
The next day her dad got it:
"You are the meanest dad in the whole wide world."

Oh, the trials and tribulations of parenting;
oh, the "slings and arrows" from one's own offspring.

After the double volley,
the meanest mom and dad in the whole world
had an evening drink, chat and a good long laugh.
They were beginning to realize that they had
the meanest little child in the whole wide world.

Mercies

In the process of letting go, you will lose many things from the past, but you will find yourself.

—Deepak Chopra

Forgiveness is not always easy. At times, it feels more painful than the wound we suffered, to forgive the one that inflicted it. And yet, there is no peace without forgiveness.

—Marianne Williamson

True forgiveness is when you can say, "Thank you for that experience."

—Oprah Winfrey

22

The Power of Forgiveness

Richard Rohr

Among the most powerful of human experiences is to give or to receive forgiveness. I want to share with you a personal story of forgiveness that happened in my family near the time of my mother's death.

She was lingering on the threshold, and for several days she had been talking about "a mesh" she couldn't get through.

I was sitting by her bed, telling her how much I would miss her. She said she wanted to hear that from my father, whom we always called "Daddy." Of course, Daddy had been telling her that for weeks.

So Daddy came over and effusively told her, "Oh, I'm going to miss ya."

She replied, "I don't believe it."

I couldn't believe my ears! I said, "Mother, you're a

few hours from death. You can't say that!"

She persisted: "I don't believe it."

Daddy redoubled his efforts: "I ask your forgiveness for all the times I've hurt you in our fifty-four years of marriage, and I forgive you for all the times you've hurt me."

I said, "Mother, isn't that beautiful? Now say that back to Daddy." And suddenly she clammed up. She didn't want to say it.

I said, "Mother, you're soon going to be before God. You don't want to come before God without forgiving everybody."

She said, "I forgive everybody."

I said, "But do you forgive Daddy?" and she became silent again.

Then Daddy jumped in and said, "Honey, I never fooled around with any other women."

We all knew that. She even said, "Well I know that, I know that."

My siblings and I still don't know how Daddy had hurt Mother. But any married person knows there are many little ways a couple can hurt one another over fifty-four years.

Then I said, "Mother, let's try this. Put one hand on your heart, and I'm going to pray that your heart gets real soft." I placed one of my hands on hers, over her heart, and held her other hand and started kissing it.

After about a minute she said, very faintly, "That melts me."

"What?"

"When you kiss my hand like that, now I've got to do it." After a pause, she continued: "I'm a stubborn woman. All of my life I've been a stubborn woman." (Mother was an Eight on the Enneagram!)

"Well, Mother, we all knew that," I said. "Now look at Daddy and you tell him."

So she looked over and she didn't call him "Daddy," as she usually did. She spoke to him by name: "Rich, I forgive you."

I prompted her again: "Mother, the other half—I ask for your forgiveness."

She started breathing heavily and rapidly. Then she summoned her energy and said, "Rich, I ask your forgiveness." A few more moments of labored breathing, and she said, "That's it, that's it. That's what I had to do."

I said to her, "Mother, do you think that was the mesh?"

She replied, "It's gone! The mesh is gone! And,

God, I pray that I mean this forgiveness from my heart."

Then she said, referring to my two sisters and my sister-in-law, "Tell the girls to do this early and not to wait 'til now. They'll understand a woman's heart and the way a man can hurt a woman."

Mother was so happy then, and fully ready for death.

That's the power and the grace of forgiveness. But let's do it now and not wait until later! Let's ask for the grace to let go of those grudges and hurts we hold on to. How else will we ever be free? In forgiveness, we live up to our true and deepest dignity. We then operate by a power and a logic not our own. We live out of the True Self and not just the tiny self that is always offended and complaining. Without forgiveness nothing new happens, and we remain frozen in a small past.

23

An Attitude of Heart

Douglas Venne, MM

In Bangladesh an owner who has more goats or cows than needed will let a poor family care for one. When I bought a goat, I asked Kangal and his wife, Khudeza, to care for it. They were very eager to do it, so I placed the animal with them. Later on, since my vacation to the United States was near, I asked Kangal if I could see the goat. "It is with my wife at her mother's place." I went there but she didn't have it. The truth came out that they had sold it. I blew my stack. Kangal and I were finished. He would get no more special consideration despite his telling me that I was his best friend.

Along came Kalu Mia. (It was Kalu, a nineteen-year-old day laborer, who had introduced me to village life when he convinced his employer to let me work in the fields.) Kalu knew the story of my goat, and he brought his friend Kangal and me together. He sat on the ground between us. On his left was Kangal, who hung his head down, and I, fuming, sat on Kalu's right. Kalu Mia said to me, "Doug, Bhai, have mercy on Kangal. Give him another chance. He will pay you all he owes."

I was astonished. Here was a Muslim preaching the gospel to me. He reminded me of how much more often than Kangal I had duped the Lord and received mercy. Mercy is not shown in an act or two. Rather, it is an attitude of heart that does not look at the balance due but at the bond needed to unite.

24

It's Never Too Late

Guy de Maupassant

She had been brought up in one of those families who live entirely to themselves, apart from all the rest of the world. Such families know nothing of political events, although they are discussed at table; for changes in the Government take place at such a distance from them that they are spoken of as one speaks of a historical event, such as the death of Louis XVI or the landing of Napoleon.

Customs are modified in course of time, fashions succeed one another, but such variations are taken no account of in the placid family circle where traditional usages prevail year after year. And if some scandalous episode or other occurs in the neighborhood, the disreputable story dies a natural death when it reaches the threshold of the house. The father and mother may, perhaps, exchange a few words on the subject when alone together some evening, but they speak in hushed tones—for even walls have ears. The father says, with bated breath:

"You've heard of that terrible affair in the Rivoil family?"

And the mother answers: "Who would have dreamed of such a thing? It's dreadful."

The children suspected nothing, and arrive in their turn at years of discretion with eyes and mind blindfolded, ignorant of the real side of life, not knowing that people do not think as they speak, and do not speak as they act; or aware that they should live at war, or at all events, in a state of armed peace, with the rest of mankind; not suspecting the fact that the simple are always deceived, the sincere made sport of, the good maltreated.

Some go on till the day of their death in this blind probity and loyalty and honor, so pure-minded that nothing can open their eyes.

Others, undeceived, but without fully understanding, make mistakes, are dismayed, and become desperate, believing themselves the playthings of a cruel fate, the wretched victims of adverse circumstances, and exceptionally wicked men.

The Savignols married their daughter Bertha

at the age of eighteen. She wedded a young Parisian, George Baron by name, who had dealings on the Stock Exchange. He was handsome, well-mannered, and apparently all that could be desired. But in the depths of his heart he somewhat despised his old-fashioned parents-in-law, whom he spoke of among his intimates as "my dear old fossils."

He belonged to a good family, and the girl was rich. They settled down in Paris. She became one of those provincial Parisians whose name is legion. She remained in complete ignorance of the great city, of its social side, its pleasures and its customs—just as she remained ignorant also of life, its perfidy, and its mysteries.

Devoted to her house, she knew scarcely anything beyond her own street; and when she ventured into another part of Paris it seemed to her that she had accomplished a long and arduous journey into some unknown, unexplored city. She would then say to her husband in the evening:

"I have been through the boulevards today."

Two or three times a year her husband took her to the theatre. These were events the remembrance of which never grew dim; they provided subjects of conversation for long afterward.

Sometimes three months afterward she would suddenly burst into laughter, and exclaim:

"Do you remember that actor dressed up as a general, who crowed like a cock?"

Her friends were limited to two families related to her own. She spoke of them as "the Martinets" and "the Michelins."

Her husband lived as he pleased, coming home when it suited him—sometimes not until dawn—alleging business, but not putting himself out overmuch to account for his movements, well aware that no suspicion would ever enter his wife's guileless soul.

But one morning she received an anonymous letter.

She was thunderstruck—too simpleminded to understand the infamy of unsigned information and to despise the letter, the writer of which declared himself inspired by interest in her happiness, hatred of evil, and love of truth.

This missive told her that her husband had had for two years past a sweetheart, a young widow named Madame Rosset, with whom he spent all his evenings.

Bertha knew neither how to dissemble her grief nor how to spy on her husband. When he came in for lunch she threw the letter down before him, burst into tears, and fled to her room.

He had time to take in the situation and to prepare his reply. He knocked at his wife's door. She opened it at once, but dared not look at him. He smiled, sat down, drew her to his knee, and in a tone of light raillery began:

"My dear child, as a matter of fact, I have a friend named Madame Rosset, whom I have known for the last ten years, and of whom I have a very high opinion. I may add that I know scores of other people whose names I have never mentioned to you, seeing that you do not care for society, or fresh acquaintan ces, or functions of any sort. But, to make short work of such vile accusations as this, I want you to put on your things after lunch, and we'll go together and call on this lady, who will very soon become a friend of yours, too, I am quite sure."

She embraced her husband warmly, and, moved by that feminine spirit of curiosity which will not be lulled once it is aroused, consented to go and see this unknown widow, of whom she was, in spite of everything, just the least bit jealous. She felt instinctively that to know a danger is to be already armed against it.

She entered a small, tastefully furnished flat on the fourth floor of an attractive house. After waiting five minutes in a drawing room rendered somewhat dark by its many curtains and hangings, a door opened, and a very dark, short, rather plump young woman appeared, surprised and smiling.

George introduced them:

"My wife—Madame Julie Rosset."

The young widow uttered a half-suppressed cry of astonishment and joy, and ran forward with hands outstretched. She had not hoped, she said, to have this pleasure, knowing that Madame Baron never saw any one, but she was delighted to make her acquaintance. She was so fond of George (she said "George" in a familiar, sisterly sort of way) that she had been most anxious to know his young wife and to make friends with her, too.

By the end of a month the two new friends were inseparable. They saw each other every day, sometimes twice a day, and dined together every evening, sometimes at one house, sometimes at the other. George no longer deserted his home, no longer talked of pressing business. He adored his own fireside, he said.

When, after a time, a flat in the house where Madame Rosset lived became vacant Madame Baron hastened to take it, in order to be near her friend and spend even more time with her than hitherto.

And for two whole years their friendship was without a cloud, a friendship of heart and mind—absolute, tender, devoted. Bertha could hardly speak without bringing in Julie's name. To her Madame Rosset represented perfection.

She was utterly happy, calm, and contented.

But Madame Rosset fell ill. Bertha hardly left her side. She spent her nights with her, distracted with grief; even her husband seemed inconsolable.

One morning the doctor, after leaving the invalid's bedside, took George and his wife aside, and told them that he considered Julie's condition very grave.

As soon as he had gone the grief-stricken husband and wife sat down opposite each other and gave way to tears. That night they both sat up with the patient. Bertha tenderly kissed her friend from time to time, while George stood at the foot of the bed, his eyes gazing steadfastly on the invalid's face.

The next day she was worse.

But toward evening she declared she felt better, and insisted that her friends should go back to their own apartment to dinner.

They were sitting sadly in the dining room, scarcely even attempting to eat, when the maid gave George a note. He opened it, turned pale as death, and, rising from the table, said to his wife in a constrained voice:

"Wait for me. I must leave you a moment. I shall be back in ten minutes. Don't go away on any account."

And he hurried to his room to get his hat.

Bertha waited for him, a prey to fresh anxiety. But, docile in everything, she would not go back to her friend till he returned.

At length, as he did not reappear, it occurred to her to visit his room and see if he had taken his gloves. This would show whether or not he had had a call to make.

She saw them at the first glance. Beside them lay a crumpled paper, evidently thrown down in haste.

She recognized it at once as the note George had received.

And a burning temptation, the first that had ever assailed her urged her to read it and discover the cause of her husband's abrupt departure. Her rebellious conscience protested but a devouring and fearful curiosity prevailed. She seized the paper, smoothed it out, recognized the tremulous, penciled writing as Julie's, and read:

"Come alone and kiss me, my poor dear. I am dying."

At first she did not understand, the idea of Julie's death being her uppermost thought. But all at once the true meaning of what she read burst in a flash upon her; this penciled note threw a lurid light upon her whole existence, revealed the whole infamous truth, all the treachery and perfidy of which she had been the victim. She understood the long years of deceit, the way in which she had been made their puppet. She saw them again, sitting side by side in the evening, reading by lamplight out of the same book, glancing at each other at the end of each page.

And her poor, indignant, suffering, bleeding heart was cast into the depths of a despair which knew no bounds.

Footsteps drew near; she fled, and shut herself in her own room.

Presently her husband called her:

"Come quickly! Madame Rosset is dying."

Bertha appeared at her door, and with trembling lips replied:

"Go back to her alone; she does not need me."

He looked at her stupidly, dazed with grief, and repeated:

"Come at once! She's dying, I tell you!"

Bertha answered:

"You would rather it were I."

Then at last he understood, and returned alone to the dying woman's bedside.

He mourned her openly, shamelessly, indifferent to the sorrow of the wife who no longer spoke to him, no longer looked at him; who passed her life in solitude, hedged round with disgust, with indignant anger, and praying night and day to God.

They still lived in the same house, however, and sat opposite each other at table, in silence and despair.

Gradually his sorrow grew less acute; but she did not forgive him.

And so their life went on, hard and bitter for them both.

For a whole year they remained as complete strangers to each other as if they had never met. Bertha nearly lost her reason.

At last one morning she went out very early, and returned about eight o'clock bearing in her hands an enormous bouquet of white roses. And she sent word to her husband that she wanted to speak to him. He came—anxious and uneasy.

"We are going out together," she said. "Please carry

these flowers; they are too heavy for me."

A carriage took them to the gate of the cemetery, where they alighted. Then, her eyes filling with tears, she said to George:

"Take me to her grave."

He trembled, and could not understand her motive; but he led the way, still carrying the flowers. At last he stopped before a white marble slab, to which he pointed without a word.

She took the bouquet from him, and, kneeling down, placed it on the grave. Then she offered up a silent, heartfelt prayer.

Behind her stood her husband, overcome by recollections of the past.

She rose, and held out her hands to him.

"If you wish it, we will be friends," she said.

Mercies

We are told that people stay in love because of chemistry, or because they remain intrigued with each other, because of many kindnesses, because of luck. But part of it has got to be forgiveness and gratefulness. —Ellen Goodman

Once a woman has forgiven her man, she must not reheat his sins for breakfast.

—Marlene Dietrich

One of the keys to happiness is a bad memory.

—Rita Mae Brown

25

Forgiveness Is a Favor We Do Ourselves

Harold Kushner

One year, my Yom Kippur sermon was on the theme of forgiveness. The next day, a woman came to see me, very upset about the sermon. She told me how, ten years earlier, her husband had left her for a younger woman and she has had to raise two children by herself for the past ten years.

She asked me angrily, "And you want me to forgive him for what he did to us?" I told her, "Yes, I want you to forgive him. Not to excuse him, not to say that what he did was acceptable, but to forgive him as a way of saying that someone who would do that has no right to live inside your head any more than he has the right to live inside your house. Why are you giving a man like that the power to turn you into a bitter, vengeful woman? He doesn't deserve that power over you."

Harold Kushner

Forgiveness is not a favor we do for the person who offended us. It is a favor we do for ourselves, cleansing our souls of thoughts and memories that lead us to see ourselves as victims and make our lives less enjoyable. When we understand we have little choice as to what other people do but we can always choose how we will respond to what they do, we can let go of those embittering memories and enter the New Year clean and fresh.

26

The Day I Stood Simmering in Shame

Brian Doyle

Committed a sin yesterday, in the hallway, at noon. I roared at my son, I grabbed him by the shirt collar, I frightened him so badly that he cowered and wept, and when he turned to run, I grabbed him by the arm so roughly that he flinched, and it was that flicker of fear and pain across his face, the bright, eager, holy-riveting face I have loved for ten years, that stopped me then and haunts me this morning, for I am the father of his fear, I sent it snarling into his heart, and I can never get it out now, which torments me.

Yes, he was picking on his brother and, yes, he had picked on his brother all morning and, yes, this was the culmination of many edgy incidents already and, no, he hadn't paid the slightest attention to warnings and remonstrations and fulminations, and, yes, he had been snide and supercilious all day, and, yes, he had deliberately done exactly the thing he had specifically been warned not to do, for murky reasons, but still, I roared at him and grabbed him and terrified him and made him cower, and now there is a dark evil wriggle between us that makes me sit here with my hands over my face, ashamed to the bottom of my bones.

I do not know how sins can be forgiven. I grasp the concept, I admire the genius of the idea, I suspect it to be the seed of all real peace, I savor the Tutus and Gandhis who have the mad courage to live by it, but I do not understand how foul can be made fair. What is done cannot be undone, and my moment of rage in the hallway is an indelible scar on his heart and mine, and while my heart is a ragged old bag after nearly half a century of slings and stings, his is still new, eager, open, suggestible, innocent; he has committed only the small sins of a child, the halting first lies, the failed test paper hidden in the closet, the window broken in petulance, the stolen candy bar, the silent witness as a classmate is bullied, the insults flung like bitter knives.

Whereas I am a man, and have had many lies squirming in my mouth, and have committed calumny, and far too often evaded the mad, ragged Christ, ignored his stink, his rotten teeth, his cloak of soggy newspapers, his voice of broken glass.

No god can forgive what we do to each other; only the injured can summon that extraordinary grace, and where such grace is born we cannot say, for all our fitful genius and miraculous machinery. We use the word god so easily, so casually, as if our label for the incomprehensible meant anything at all; and we forget all too easily that the wriggle of holy is born only through the stammer and stumble of us, who are always children. So we turn again and again to each other, and bow, and ask forgiveness, and mill what mercy we can muster from the muddle of our hearts.

The instant I let go of my son's sinewy arm in the hallway, he sprinted away and slammed the door and flew off the porch and ran down the street, and I stood there simmering in shame. Then I walked down the hill into the laurel thicket as dense and silent as the dawn of the world and found him there huddled and sobbing. We sat in the moist, green dark for a long time, not saying anything, the branches burly and patient. Finally, I asked quietly for his forgiveness and he asked for mine and we walked out of the woods, hand in hand, changed men.

27

What Kind of People Are These?

Joan Chittister

The country that went through the rabid slaughter of children at Columbine high school several years ago once again stood stunned at the rampage in a tiny Amish school this month. We were, in fact, more than unusually saddened by this particular display of viciousness. It was, of course, an attack on ten little girls. Amish. Five dead. Five wounded. Most people called it "tragic." After all, the Amish represent no threat to society, provide no excuse for the rationalization of the violence so easily practiced by the world around them. Nevertheless, in a nation steeped in violence—from its video games to its military history, in foreign policy and on its streets—the question remains: Why did this particular disaster affect us like it did? You'd think we'd be accustomed to mayhem by now.

But there was something different about this one. What was it?

Make no mistake about it: the Amish are not strangers to violence.

The kind of ferocity experienced by the Amish as they buried the five girl-children murdered by a crazed gunman two weeks ago has not really been foreign to Amish life and the history of this peaceful people.

This is a people born out of opposition to violence—and, at the same time, persecuted by both Catholics and Protestants in the era before religious tolerance. Having failed to adhere to the orthodoxy of one or the other of the controlling theocracies of their home territories, they were banished, executed, imprisoned, drowned, or burned at the stake by both groups.

But for over three hundred years, they have persisted in their intention to be who and what they said they were.

Founded by a once-Catholic priest in the late seventeenth century, as part of the reformist movements of the time, the Mennonites—from which the Amish later sprung—were, from the beginning, a simple movement. They believe in adult baptism, pacifism, religious tolerance, separation of church and state, opposition to capital punishment, and opposition to oaths and civil office.

They organize themselves into local house churches. They separate from the "evil" of the world around them. They live simple lives opposed to the technological devices—and even the changing clothing styles—which, in their view, encourage the individualism, the pride, that erodes community, family, a righteous society. They work hard. They're self-sufficient; they refuse both Medicare and Social Security monies from the state. And though the community has suffered its own internal violence from time to time, they have inflicted none on anyone around them.

Without doubt, to see such a peaceful people brutally attacked would surely leave any decent human being appalled.

But it was not the violence suffered by the Amish community last week that surprised people. Our newspapers are full of brutal and barbarian violence day after day after day—both national and personal.

No, what really stunned the country about the attack on the small Amish schoolhouse in Pennsylvania was that the Amish community itself simply refused to hate what had hurt them.

"Do not think evil of this man," the Amish grandfather told his children at the mouth of one little girl's grave.

"Do not leave this area. Stay in your home here," the Amish delegation told the family of the murderer. "We forgive this man."

No, it was not the murders, not the violence, that shocked us; it was the forgiveness that followed it for which we were not prepared. It was the lack of recrimination, the dearth of vindictiveness that left us amazed. Baffled. Confounded.

It was the Christianity we all profess but which they practiced that left us stunned. Never had we seen such a thing.

Here they were, those whom our Christian ancestors called "heretics," who were modeling Christianity for all the world to see. The whole lot of them. The entire community of them. Thousands of them at one time.

The real problem with the whole situation is that down deep we know that we had the chance to do the same. After the fall of the Twin Towers we had the sympathy, the concern, the support of the entire world.

You can't help but wonder, when you see something like this, what the world would be like today if, instead of using the fall of the Twin Towers as an excuse to invade a nation, we had simply gone to every Muslim country on Earth and said, "Don't be afraid. We won't hurt you. We know that this is coming from only a fringe of society, and we ask your help in saving others from this same kind of violence."

"Too idealistic," you say. Maybe. But since we didn't try, we'll never know, will we?

Instead, we have sparked fear of violence in the rest of the world ourselves. So much so, that they are now making nuclear bombs to save themselves. From whom? From us, of course.

The record is clear. Instead of exercising more vigilance at our borders, listening to our allies and becoming more of what we say we are, we are becoming who they said we are.

For the 3,000 dead in the fall of the Twin Towers at the hands of 19 religious fanatics, we have more than 2,700 U.S. soldiers now killed in military action, more than 20,600 wounded, more than 10,000 permanently disabled. We have thousands of widows and orphans, a constitution at risk, a president that asked for and a Congress that just voted to allow torture, and a national infrastructure in jeopardy for want of future funding.

And nobody's even sure how many thousand innocent Iraqis are dead now, too.

Indeed, we have done exactly what the terrorists wanted us to do. We have proven that we are the oppressors, the exploiters, the demons they now fear we are. And—read the international press—few people are saying otherwise around the world.

From where I stand, it seems to me that we ourselves are no longer so sure just exactly what kind of people we have now apparently become.

Interestingly enough, we do know what kind of people the Amish are—and, like the early Romans, we, too, are astounded at it. "Christian" they call it.

A Mercy

To be a Christian means to forgive the inexcusable, because God has forgiven the inexcusable in you.

This is hard. It is perhaps not so hard to forgive a single great injury. But to forgive the incessant provocations of daily life—to keep on forgiving the bossy mother-in-law, the bullying husband, the nagging wife, the selfish daughter, the deceitful son—how can we do it? Only, I think, by remembering where we stand, by meaning our words when we say in our prayers each night 'forgive our trespasses as we forgive those that trespass against us.' We are offered forgiveness on no other terms. To refuse it is to refuse God's mercy for ourselves. There is no hint of exceptions and God means what He says.

—C. S. Lewis

28

Punched in the Stomach

Alice Camille

As much as I don't want to forgive Warren Hunt for punching me in the stomach every day of kindergarten I totally *don't want to forgive Miss Kiley for not moving my seat.*

On the first day of kindergarten, Warren Hunt punched me in the stomach. You'd think I wouldn't remember the name of a five-year-old villain for over half a century, but you'd be wrong. I owe Warren Hunt a punch in the stomach—and if he shows up today I'm going to make him one *sorry* middle-aged man.

You might wonder what I did to deserve a punch. All I did was sit next to a boy I didn't know in the circle of seats around our teacher Miss Kiley. I figured she didn't see when the strange boy hauled off and hit me with his fist. And warned me not to say anything, or he'd punch me again.

It might seem petty, remembering a punch in the stomach from all the way back in kindergarten. But it wasn't just a punch. The next day Miss Kiley told us to take the same seats as the day before. She told us these were our assigned seats for the year. So I sat next to this boy Warren Hunt again—and he punched me again. And warned me not to tell, and I didn't. This went on all year. So now when I think of kindergarten, I remember making turkey drawings with our hands and learning how to print my name. And being punched in the stomach every single day by Warren Hunt.

I became scared to go to school, as you can imagine. I loved learning things, and story time, and playing in the big toy room. But I feared sitting in that circle and being slugged. I told my mom: "My stomach hurts at school."

"Why?" she asked. "I thought you liked Miss Kiley."

"I do like Miss Kiley," I confessed. "But I'm afraid of Warren Hunt." So I told Mom what was happening in the circle, and she told me to tell the teacher.

I was happy to go to school the next day. I thought my mother had come up with a wonderful answer to my problem. I went right up to Miss Kiley the next day and whispered in her ear, "Warren Hunt punches me in the stomach." To my amazement, she replied, "I know. I'm sorry about that."

I was speechless. Neither my mother nor I had conceived any scenario that included this information. Nor was I prepared when Miss Kiley continued, "You see, honey, Warren's parents are *di-vor-cing*." She whispered the word slowly to me as if it were the name of a rare disease that should inspire my pity. Back in 1963, divorce was a rare disease and it did inspire pity. But I was having a hard time connecting the dots between Warren's parents . . . and my stomach. I could see that if Warren's parents didn't love each other anymore, that would be sad and scary for him. But he was punching *me*. And my mom was depending on me to straighten this out.

I tried again. "Could you change my seat?" I asked Miss Kiley, as sweetly as I could.

"If I change your seat," Miss Kiley said, "He'll just punch some other little girl." My perception of the world shifted on its axis. This was how life was. Nothing would be done. Warren was going to punch SOMEONE so it might as well be me. My teacher was offering me up as a sacrifice to a wounded boy.

She didn't know how to stop it, and I didn't have the power to. For the rest of the year, I absorbed the frustration of a boy living in a broken home.

In kindergarten, I learned how to print my name, and another really important lesson I never forgot: Angry people are bound to hit someone—so it might as well be you.

We all know forgiveness is a task we have to engage. It's the central task of living in a broken, sinful, imperfect world. But how do we get from injustice to forgiveness? It's tough to forgive your trespassers while they're still dancing in your front yard. When the person who's hurt you has yet to say they're sorry.

For the record, Warren Hunt never said he was sorry. Miss Kiley did; but I didn't believe her. Because she was the grownup. It was her job to protect me and she wasn't good at it. I spent nine months being a punching bag for an angry kid, and as much as I don't want to forgive Warren Hunt, I totally don't want to forgive Miss Kiley.

What was her problem? Was she a new teacher who didn't have a clue how to handle the situation? Or was she simply—like many of us—just not as personally resourceful as her job required her to be? Today's helicopter parents would swarm into a classroom like hers with lawyers in tow. But the 1960s were an age when parents respected a teacher's sovereign right to rule the classroom. My mom was a woman with five other kids to mind. So Mom did nothing. Should I add Mom to the list of folks I refuse to forgive?

And why stop there? My fourth grade teacher once shamed me in front of the whole class. Because of that experience, I was paralyzed at the thought of standing in front of a group for the next twenty years! My crime, as I recall, was "being sneaky." Well, guess what? I'm still pretty sneaky! So all that drama back in the fourth grade didn't even accomplish what it set out to do: to blot out my incarnate badness.

My incarnate badness, by the way, is the point of the creation story in Genesis. Not just MY incarnate badness, but yours too. Our mutual inescapable propensity to badness warrants a whole doctrine of the church: Original Sin. Which says, basically, that whether you and I happen to be punch-ees or punch-ers at any given situation in life, neither of us is innocent. Because given the chance, you or I would quickly change sides and forsake our innocence for the next good punch. Speaking of which, when Warren Hunt turns up in my life again, we'll find out how innocent I am. You just watch.

On my list of unforgivables, do include my eighth

grade English teacher. She accused me of plagiarism. She said I wasn't capable of writing the composition I handed in: I wasn't smart enough to write an essay that good, she said. So she gave me a D. This time, my mother went to bat for me. She told the teacher I wrote that composition in her presence while she was ironing! The teacher, out of spite for the trouble I caused her, gave me a D anyway—because of a single run-on sentence. I'd like to tell that English teacher I've since made a career of writing run-on sentences, I get PAID for writing run-on sentences, and have in fact made it my mission in life to rehabilitate the reputation of run-on sentences—like this one. I win awards for writing run-on sentences, I would tell her. But I bet she'd still give me a D. She'd give me a D for this story, I bet. Maybe you would too.

I know I have to reconcile this business with Warren Hunt, and Miss Kiley, and the shaming fourth grade teacher (who was right about me being sneaky), and the accusing eighth grade teacher, who was wrong about the plagiarism. I should probably even go back and forgive Warren Hunt's PARENTS for divorcing in the first place. I don't know for sure if Warren's life would have been better—or mine, for that matter. Maybe Warren would have turned out to be a punching boy anyway. But at least Miss Kiley might have changed my seat!

I want to learn to forgive poor Warren Hunt, who punched his way through kindergarten—and may be punching still. But it's not just him, I realize; the same violence that blossomed in that wounded child lives in me too. My heart harbors its own menace that springs up in surprising hours, whenever I feel the need to defend myself. That may be how life is. But it's not how it has to be. In the hour of greatest personal peril, Jesus ordered his friends to put their swords away. I want mine handy. Because I don't know yet how to live in the world without one.

I've come to suspect that forgiveness is not a matter of church theology and sacramental formulas. It turns out to be a deeply personal business. It's about Warren and the teachers and Mom and me. You and I have to find a way through the darkness of history—and our own unique histories—and there's only one way. There has always been one way. We have to forgive as we're forgiven—or we're lost.

Holy Mary, mother of God, pray for *this* sinner, now and at the hour of my death. And especially now—so when I meet Warren again, I can get it right.

29

Forgive

Maya Angelou

Take me, Virginia,
bind me close
with Jamestown memories
of camptown races and
ships pregnant
with certain cargo
and Richmond riding high on greed
and low on tedious tides
of guilt.
But take me on, Virginia,
loose your turban of flowers
that peach petals and
dogwood bloom may
form epaulettes of white
tenderness on my shoulders
and round my

The Way of Forgiveness

head ringlets
of forgiveness, poignant
as rolled eyes, sad as summer
parasols in a hurricane.

Part Three
THE FORGIVENESS OF OTHERS

The Lord Is Merciful and Gracious

Psalm 103:8–12

The LORD is merciful and gracious,
slow to anger and abounding in steadfast love.
He will not always accuse,
nor will he keep his anger forever.
He does not deal with us according to our sins,
nor repay us according to our iniquities.
For as the heavens are high above the earth,
so great is his steadfast love toward those who
fear him;
as far as the east is from the west,
so far he removes our transgressions from us.

30

Forgiveness Is the Only Way to Begin

Michael Leach

This letter from Michael Leach was first sent by mail to Pope Francis in March 2013, when the pope was inaugurated and then appeared as an open letter in the National Catholic Reporter *on April 9. Two years later on April 10, 2015 Pope Francis announced a Holy Year of Mercy. "Let us not forget that God forgives and God forgives always," he said. "Let us never tire of asking for forgiveness."*

Dear Father Francis,

If I may, I address you as Father rather than Your Holiness because when you were cardinal you asked your flock to call you Father rather than Your Eminence. What a beautiful symbol that word can be! I was blessed with a father who loved me unconditionally and taught me by his example what it means to pray to God as "Our Father."

You also rode a bus throughout Buenos Aires, Argentina, to visit the sick, feed the hungry, and go to work. You must have received words of gratitude, plenty of requests, and lots of suggestions from your traveling companions. This letter from a fellow traveler on the way is in gratitude for the example of your simplicity and also a suggestion. Please consider it.

Begin your new vocation as leader of the church with a worldwide Forgiveness Mass. Forgiveness is the only way to begin anew, and you have proven how much you appreciate its healing value. I loved reading how after you became pope you urged confessors in the basilica to "be merciful—the souls of the faithful need your mercy." It's clear you are a pastor who treasures the words of Jesus to his disciples: "I desire mercy and not sacrifice" (Matthew 12:7). In your first sermon you shared the story of a very old woman who taught you, "The Lord forgives everything." As archbishop, you scolded those priests who refused to baptize the babies of unwed mothers. You also knelt at the deathbed of a bishop who had left the church in scandal to marry, who had become poor and alone, and you comforted him. You even joked with the cardinals who had elected you pope, "May God forgive you for what you have done!" You know the power of forgiveness.

I suggest that you propose a Forgiveness Sunday, as soon as possible in every church in the world where each of us can ask for forgiveness and give forgiveness and receive forgiveness through a general absolution. A month after your announcement, it can happen something like this:

Every church has set up television screens at the sides of the altar, or radio speakers. You are presiding at the same Forgiveness Mass in St. Peter's Basilica that is televised to the churches and the world.

You and the ministers lead the people in prayer: "I confess to Almighty God . . . "

At the end of the Confiteor those of us in the pews observe your face on TV as you ask forgiveness on behalf of the church for all those it has hurt, living and dead. You acknowledge the church's sins against children, and beg forgiveness from them and their families, in the heart of Jesus. You also ask for and give forgiveness to all the women and men who did not have the means to get annulments and so divorced and remarried, and encourage them to receive Communion again, no strings attached. This is something you have dreamed of doing for a long time, and it is clear: "Now is the acceptable time!" (2 Corinthians 6:2).

You ask each of us to recognize and regret our own sins, and redirect ourselves to God who is unconditional love. We bow our heads and recognize our wasted angers, our sad lusts, our worthless greed, and become aware that we still hold others, living or dead, in bondage to resentments. We confess our darkness to God and lay our sins on the altar of Love where they immediately become "as white as snow" (Isaiah 1:18).

"Lord, have mercy . . . Christ, have mercy . . . Lord, have mercy . . ."

The lectors read: "Neither death nor life, nor angels nor principalities nor powers, nor things present nor things to come, nor height nor depth, nor any other created thing, shall be able to separate us from the love of God which is in Christ Jesus our Lord!" (Romans 8:38–39).

The deacons read the Gospel of the adulteress whom Jesus saved from stoning.

Then, Father Francis, you speak and remind us as you did in your first Sunday sermon as pope, of the breathtaking truth that we can never hear enough: When Jesus gave the adulteress new life, he didn't say,

"Sin no more and I will not condemn you." He said, "I do not condemn you. Now go and sin no more." We first experience God's love, and then our life changes forever. "Mercy," you said, "is the Lord's most powerful message." Love begins with forgiveness, unearned and freely given. It is the meaning of Christ's life, death and resurrection.

At the Lord's Prayer, everyone looks at their neighbor and says, "Forgive me." Forgiveness received, they say in kind, "I forgive you." They embrace. The world embraces.

Before Communion you grant a general absolution to all of God's children in all the churches in all the world. Forgiveness becomes an almighty force that opens hearts, cleanses minds, and inspires action. Just like Mary Magdalene, we are free to go and sin no more! Everybody starts from scratch. This is the only way the church—or anyone—can be born again.

In Eucharist we then share with gratitude the one body of Christ of which we are inseparable members (1 Corinthians 12:12–14).

At the end of the Mass you tell us all, "Go and give what God has given you!"

Forgiveness becomes a theme of our lives. The church can now ask forgiveness of those it has marginalized, judged and condemned with verbal stones. It announces God's love and forgiveness of every woman, living or dead, who has made the gut-wrenching, life-shattering decision to have an abortion. Catholics everywhere tire of blaming those who disagree or dissent or are different, and set them free by no longer holding them hostage in their consciousness. Free again. Free to be loved and love again. By practicing what it preaches, the church not only draws more people to a loving God but is now able to reach out to other religions without wanting anything in return.

Little miracles begin to happen. Liberal reform groups invite members of conservative groups to engage in dialogue at conferences. They eat together. Forgiveness is an energy, and energy transforms itself into other forms of energy: words, behaviors, healings. People treat each other with respect. Peace extinguishes anger, love overcomes fear. The consciousness of forgiveness becomes a collective consciousness, and someday, who knows, the Cosmic Consciousness it always is but we didn't recognize because we failed to accept and affirm the forgiveness that has always been ours. And someday, who knows, the words of Teilhard de Chardin, will come to life:

"Someday, after mastering the winds, the waves, the tides, and gravity, we shall harness for God the energies of love, and then, for a second time in the history of the world, man will have discovered fire!"

With love in Christ,
Michael Leach

31

The First Step of Forgiveness

Henri Nouwen

Forgiveness is made possible by the knowledge that human beings cannot offer us what only God can give. Once we have heard the voice calling us the Beloved, accepted the gift of full communion, and claimed the first unconditional love, we can see easily—with the eyes of a repentant heart—how we have demanded of people a love that only God can give. It is the knowledge of that first love that allows us to forgive those who have only a "second" love to offer.

I am struck by how I cling to my own wounded self. Why do I think so much about the people who have offended or hurt me? Why do I allow them to have so much power over my feelings and emotions? Why can't I simply be grateful for the good they did and forget about their failures and mistakes? It seems that in order to find my place in life I need to be angry, resentful, or hurt. It even seems that these people gave me my identity by the very ways in which they wounded me. Part of me is "the wounded one." It is hard to know who I am when I can no longer point my finger at someone who is the cause of my pain!

It is important to understand our suffering. It is often necessary to search for the origins of our mental and emotional struggles and to discover how other people's actions and our response to their actions have shaped the way we think, feel, and act. Most of all, it is freeing to become aware that we do not have to be victims of our past and can learn new ways of responding. But there is a step beyond the recognition and identification of the facts of life. There is even a step beyond choosing how to live our own life story. It is the greatest step a human being can take. It is the step of forgiveness.

Forgiveness is the name of love practiced among people who love poorly. The hard truth is that all of us love poorly. We do not even know what we are doing when we hurt others. We need to forgive and be forgiven every day, every hour—unceasingly. That is the great work of love among the fellowship of the weak that is the human family. The voice that calls us the Beloved is the voice of freedom because it sets us free to love without wanting anything in return. This has nothing to do with self-sacrifice, self-denial, or self-deprecation. But it has everything to do with the abundance of love that has been freely given to me and from which I freely want to give.

32

The Miracle of the Butterfly

Gerald G. Jampolsky

Letting go and forgiveness are one and the same.
Their function is to let emotional attachment and
investment in the past dissolve.
Their purpose is to let us experience
Oneness with God.
When applied to "special relationships," letting go
and forgiveness permit us to free ourselves
from the imprisonment in someone else, under the
guise that the other person has something we need.
Letting go and forgiveness are like
transcending the barriers and limitations of the
cocoon, to become the essence of joy and freedom
and beauty that we see in the butterfly.
It is the Oneness we see when
the color and hues of the butterfly's wings
blend imperceptibly with a vibrant flower.
It allows us to experience the essence of our own love

as One with everything in the Universe.
When we let go and forgive
in a special relationship, we experience
the miracle of immediately dissolving
jealousy, possessiveness, exclusiveness,
and the feelings of "missing."
The feeling of wanting to
get something from another person;
the need to control, manipulate, and
predict the behavior of another person,
simply vanishes.
The love/hate of special relationships,
hating or loving according to whether
one's imagined needs are met or not,
also disappears.
The result of this miracle is that we remember and
recognize that our only essence is Love,
and Love needs nothing: its only function is to
self-create.
The miracle of the butterfly is symbolically the
transformation of a special relationship into
a Holy One, through letting go of the chains
of our self-imposed imprisonment.
The miracle of the butterfly is the knowledge that
we are One with each other and with God forever.

A Mercy

Forgiveness is a strange thing. It can sometimes be easier to forgive our enemies than our friends. It can be hardest of all to forgive people we love. Like all of life's important coping skills, the ability to forgive and the capacity to let go of resentments most likely take root very early in our lives.

—Mr. Rogers

33

The Plus Sign

Julie Schumacher Cohen

As we enter deeper into Lent and continue to abstain from certain foods and habits, even those who have given up constantly checking Facebook and Twitter cannot retreat entirely from our divided, toxic political environment.

Partly because of my work in community and government relations for a Jesuit university, and partly the responsibility of simply being a citizen I will continue to take in news. This means I will inevitably be exposed to the usual mix of "fake news," political grandstanding, and negative partisanship—what the Stanford political scientists Shanto Iyengar and Masha Krupenkin call "a primal sense of 'us against them.'"

Can our preparations for Easter help us cope with this reality? Can they do so not only now, but throughout the year?

In the Eastern Orthodox tradition in which I worship, the season of Lent begins with a "Forgiveness Vespers." At the end of the service, each member of the community proceeds to the front of the church to exchange with the priest and fellow parishioners—the whole church—a plea of repentance.

One by one, you bow to the person before you and then, coming face to face, you say: "Forgive me!" The other person responds: "God forgives. I forgive." You then extend your hand and the kiss of peace (or two or three, depending on the parish). And so it goes until each person has asked every other person for forgiveness, and the entire church is encircling the sanctuary. Like a lot of Eastern liturgy, this service is touchy-feely. There are giggly kids and generous grandmas. There are self-conscious teenagers, people with bad breath and sometimes tears. My cheeks usually feel a bit scratchy and irritated by the end.

In those brief exchanges, we are not able to work out all of the sins and slights that may have built up over the year, and we are not able to test the sincerity of the other's plea. Is it possible to just go through the motions? Yes. Has all truly been forgiven and made right? Maybe not.

Nonetheless, it is an important and visceral step toward the other: an invitation to and entering in of

God's grace. It is remarkable just how much is communicated in that awkward, emotional, and hope-filled receiving line. Holding a gaze with your fellow church members for those brief seconds, there is a searing sensation. You remember back to the exact moment (or moments) over the last twelve months when you were short-tempered or selfish or uncaring—forgetting to inquire after an ill parishioner's health, interpreting a turned head as judgment of my unruly five-year-old's noisemaking.

Whatever is going on in the world around us, and in our own little worlds, this ritual breaks in with a reminder of transformational love and the possibility of reconciliation. This year more than most, I wished there was a way to bring the annual Lenten practice to my social media feeds and to our country.

On Forgiveness Sunday, we look for the best in the one we forgive and seek to give a charitable interpretation of the other's intent—what Jesuits call the "plus sign," in reference to Annotation 22 of St. Ignatius' *Spiritual Exercises*. In contrast, fake news—and the hyper-partisan confirmation bias that helps to fuel it—is almost always about making the other seem worse than he or she actually is.

In his message for World Communications Day

2018, Pope Francis wrote that fake news grabs people's attention "by appealing to stereotypes and common social prejudices, and exploiting instantaneous emotions like anxiety, contempt, anger and frustration." He identifies the "tragedy of disinformation" as one that "discredits others, presenting them as enemies, to the point of demonizing them and fomenting conflict."

Similarly, Arthur Brooks, the president of the American Enterprise Institute, observed, "If we want to solve the problem of polarization today, we have to solve the contempt problem." The contempt that infects our political discourse, he said, stems from "the utter conviction of the worthlessness of another human being."

Findings from Pew Research Center back up this observation. In 2017, 44 percent of Democrats and 45 percent of Republicans had a "very unfavorable" view of members of the other party—up from just 20 percent on both sides in 1994.

Mr. Brooks, who counts the Dalai Lama among his friends, asked the Buddhist spiritual leader for advice: "What do I do when I feel contempt?" The Dalai Lama's answer: "Practice warm-heartedness." In my parish on Forgiveness Sunday, we engaged in some of that practice through a liturgical exchange of mutual repentance and connection.

While the ritual is certainly not designed to decrease the dissemination of fake news or break down political echo chambers, it could help us see a way forward from our bitter polarization. As we proceed through Lent, we might ask ourselves if we would make a sensational or questionable or mocking claim about another person if, instead of sitting behind a screen, we had to stand face to face with our "friends" or "followers."

Proximity matters. I know it did on that Sunday with those I bowed to and kissed and hugged—brought through physical nearness to encounter others as God would have me see them. Perhaps this Lenten practice should not be left for just once a year.

34

Forgiveness Sunday

Metropolitan Anthony of Sourozh

Forgiveness comes at the moment when we say to one another: I recognize your frailty, I see how deeply you wound me, and because I am wounded, because I am a victim—at times guilty, and at times innocent—I can turn to God, and from the depth of pain and of agony, of shame, and at times of despair, I can say to the Lord: Lord—forgive! He does not know what he is doing! If he only knew how deeply wounding his words are, if he only knew how destructive he is for me in my life, he would not do it. But he is blind, he is immature, he is frail; and I accept his frailty, and I will carry him, or her, as a good shepherd carries the lost sheep; because we are all lost sheep of the fold of Christ. Or else, if necessary, I will carry him, or her, or them as Christ carried his cross—to the point of death, to the point of love crucified, to the point when all power of forgiveness is given if we only have accepted to forgive whatever was done to us.

And so let us enter into this Lent, as one moves from darkness into twilight, and from twilight into light: with joy and light in our hearts, shaking off our feet the dust of the earth, shaking off all the fetters that make us prisoners—prisoners of greed, of envy, of fear, of hatred, of jealousy, prisoners of our lack of mutual understanding, prisoners of our self-centeredness because we live like prisoners within ourselves and we are called by God to be free. Then we will see how step after step we move as though it were across the vast sea, away from the earth of darkness and twilight toward the divine light; we will meet the Crucifix, and we will meet one day at the end of it love divine revealed to us in its tragic perfection before it reaches us as an unutterable glory and joy. First, Passion Week, first the cross; and then the wonder of resurrection. We must enter into both, enter into the Passion of Christ together with him, and enter together with him into the great peace and into the shining light of the resurrection.

For myself, I will ask forgiveness of you for all that I have not done that should have been done, for the awkward way in which I do things, and for the many,

many things that should be done and are never done.

But let us now support one another on this journey by mutual forgiveness, by love, remembering that very often on a hard journey it is the people from whom we expect nothing good that at a moment of crisis will stretch out a supportive hand—people whom we thought were alien to us, or inimical, who suddenly will see our need and meet it. So let us open our hearts, our minds and eyes and be ready to see and to respond.

Let us now begin by going to the icon of Christ, our God and our Savior, who paid a heavy price to have power to forgive; let us turn to the Mother of God who has given her only begotten Son for our salvation; if she can forgive—who would refuse forgiveness to us?

And then turn to one another. While we come we will hear no longer songs of repentance, but as though they were coming from afar off, the hymns of the resurrection that will grow stronger halfway to the Feast of the Cross, and will fill this church and indeed the world in the night when Christ was raised and his victory won. Amen.

Mercies

Mercy is a sweet gracious working in love, mingled with plenteous pity: for mercy worketh in keeping us, and mercy worketh turning to us all things to good.

—Julian of Norwich

Forgiveness is the final form of love.

—Reinhold Niebuhr

To forgive is the highest, most beautiful form of love. In return, you will receive untold peace and happiness.

—Robert Muller

35

Jesus Challenges Us

William F. Mullan, MM

And that is how my heavenly Father will deal with you unless you forgive your brother from your heart.
—Matthew 18:35

In August 1981 I went up from Guatemala City to San Mateo Ixtatan in Huehuetengo, a drive of about eight hours. I had been pastor there for six years before I was elected to be the regional superior for the Maryknoll Society in Central America, which required that I move down to Guatemala City. Fr. Ron Hennessey, the former regional superior, then took my place in San Mateo parish. He had mailed me a copy of an article he had written describing the recent massacres of almost one thousand Mayan Chuj-speaking people in the different villages of the parish. At his request we sent the description to one of his sisters, a nun in the United States. She submitted it to several newspapers, and it was widely published.

Now I was returning to San Mateo to visit Ron and the people. I knew it would be a difficult visit and that Ron would be in danger from the military, who had to be very angry with him for sending out his report. These were also people I loved to be with and serve, and I had known many of those who had been massacred.

While I was standing outside the four-hundred-year-old church, I saw about twenty soldiers holding Israeli machine guns just across the road. They were standing there with chickens, pigs, horses, and several small radios around them. Ron had told me that they were selling what they had looted after the massacres. I stood there and for the first time in my life I began to have feelings of hatred.

Tumik, a Mayan woman of about sixty years, came over to me and said simply, "Father, they are our brothers. I would give them a glass of water if they asked." Tumik had become a member of the Catholic Church while I was pastor there. I turned away from the scene and with Tumik went into the church to concelebrate a Mass with Ron for the dead and for the soldiers. Jesus does challenge us with "love your enemies"!

36

God the Forgiver: Forgiveness and Repentance in Islam

Muzammil Siddiqi

God has granted intellect to human beings. The intellect entails responsibility. The more intellect a person has, the more he/she is responsible.

When the intellect is missing, the responsibility is also not there. Little children are not held responsible, because their intellect has not yet developed. The insane are not responsible, because they have lost the intellectual capacity. However, part of our being human is also that we make mistakes. Sometimes we make mistakes without deliberation and intention. But sometimes we knowingly and deliberately sin and do wrong to others.

It is said: "To err is human and to forgive is divine." Both parts of this statement are very true. As human beings we are responsible, but we do also make mistakes and we are constantly in need of forgiveness. Islam speaks about two elements of forgiveness: a) God's forgiveness; b) human forgiveness. We need both, because we do wrong in our relations to God as well as in our relations to each other.

There are many names of God given in the Qur'an. They are called "Most beautiful names" and they indicate many different and diverse attributes and qualities of God. Some of these names are related to His mercy and forgiveness. Let us look at some of these names:

1. *Al-Ghafoor (The Most Forgiving):* This name occurs in the Qur'an more than seventy times. There are other names from the same root, such as Ghafir and Ghaffar. The meaning of the Arabic word "ghafara" is to cover, to hide, and from it comes the meaning "to excuse," "to pardon," "to remit," and "to forgive." God does all these things. In the Qur'an, it is mentioned that God does not forgive the Shirk (without repentance) but he may forgive every other sin for whomsoever he wills (4:116). We must turn to God to seek his forgiveness.

2. *Al-`Afuw (The Pardoner):* This is another part of forgiveness. This name occurs in the Qur'an five times. Literally, the word "'Afw" means "to release," "to heal," "to restore," "to remit." Thus, in relation

to God it means "to release us from the burden of punishment due to our sins and mistakes; to restore our honor after we have dishonored ourselves by committing sins and making mistakes." Sometimes in the Qur'an both names, Afuw and Ghafoor, come together.

3. *Al-Tawwab (The Acceptor of Repentance):* This name of God is mentioned in the Qur'an about eleven times. Allah accepts repentance of those who sincerely repent and turn to him. The word "tawwab" gives the sense of "oft-returning," which means that he again and again accepts the repentance. We make sins and mistakes then we repent, he accepts our repentance. Then again, we commit sins and make mistakes and when we repent, he again very kindly accepts us and gives us another chance.

4. *Al-Haleem (The Clement):* This name is mentioned fifteen times in the Qur'an. This means that God is not quick to judgment. He gives time. He forbears and is patient to see his servant return to him.

5. *Al-Rahman and Al-Rahim (The Most Merciful and Compassionate):* These names are the most frequent in the Qur'an. Al-Rahman is mentioned 57 times and al-Raheem is mentioned 115 times. Al-Rahman indicates that God's mercy is abundant

and plenty and Al-Raheem indicates that this is always the case with God. God is full of love and mercy and is ever Merciful.

The Qur'an teaches that God is a judge and he also punishes, but God is not bound to punish. The justice of God, according to the Qur'an, is that God does not and will not inflict undue punishment on any person. He will not ignore the good of any person. But if he wishes to forgive any sinner, he has full freedom to do that. His mercy is unlimited and his love is infinite.

There are many verses in the Qur'an and sayings of the Prophet Muhammad (peace be upon him) on God's love, mercy, and forgiveness. In one of the prayers that the Prophet taught, he said: "O God, You are most Forgiving One, You love to forgive, so forgive me" (At-Trimidhi & Ibn Majah). We need God's mercy and forgiveness all the time. It is wrong to assume at any time that one will find eternal salvation without the forgiveness of God.

Just as it is important to believe in God's mercy and forgiveness, it is also necessary to base human relations on forgiveness. We cannot expect God's forgiveness unless we also forgive those who do wrong to us. Forgiving each other, even forgiving one's enemies, is one of the most important of Islamic teachings. In the Qur'an, God has described the Believers as: "those who avoid major sins and acts of indecencies and when they are angry they forgive" (42:37).

In the same chapter, God says: "The reward of the evil is the evil thereof, but whosoever forgives and makes amends, his reward is upon God" (42:40). In another place the Qur'an says: "If you punish, then punish with the like of that wherewith you were afflicted. But if you endure patiently, indeed it is better for the patient. Endure you patiently. Your patience is not except through the help of God . . ." (16:126–27). In one the famous sayings of the Prophet (peace be upon him) it is reported that he said that God commanded him about nine things. One of them he mentioned was "that I forgive those who do wrong to me."

Prophet Muhammad was the most forgiving person. He was ever ready to forgive his enemies. When he went to Ta'if to preach God's message to its people, they mistreated him. They abused him and hit him with stones. He left the city humiliated and wounded. When he took shelter under a tree, God's angel appeared to him and told him that God was very angry with the people of Ta'if and sent him to destroy them because they mistreated God's beloved Prophet. The

Prophet prayed to God to save the people of Ta'if, because what they did was out of their ignorance. He said: "O Allah, guide these people, because they did not know what they were doing" (Al-Bukhari).

When he entered the city of Makkah (Mecca) after the victory, the Prophet had in front of him some of his staunchest enemies. Those who fought him for many years, persecuted his followers and killed many of them. Now he had full power to do whatever he wanted to punish them for their crimes. It is reported that the Prophet asked them: "What do you think I shall do to you now?" They expected nothing but retaliation and pleaded for mercy. The Prophet said, "Today I shall say to you what Yusuf (Prophet Joseph) said to his brothers: 'No blame on you today. Go, you are all free'" (Al-Albani).

Soon they all came and accepted Islam at his hands. He forgave even Hend who had caused the murder of his uncle Hamza. After killing him, she had his body mutilated and chewed his liver. When she accepted Islam, the Prophet even forgave her.

A very striking example of forgiveness we find in the Qur'an is in reference to the most unfortunate event of the "Slander of Aisha." Some hypocrites of Madinah accused her: They tried to sully her noble character. One of the slanderers turned out to be Mistah, the cousin of Aisha's father Abu Bakr. Abu Bakr used to give financial help to this young man. After he slandered his daughter, Abu Bakr vowed not to help him anymore. But God reminded Abu Bakr and through him all the Believers: "Let not those among you who are endued with grace and amplitude of means resolve by oath against helping their kinsmen, those in want and those who migrated in the path of God. Let them forgive and overlook. Do you not wish that God should also forgive you. Indeed God is Oft-Forgiving, Most Merciful" (24: 22).

Abu Bakr came out of his home and said: "Yes, indeed, I do want God's forgiveness. He did not only continue to help him but he increased his allowance. Islam emphasizes justice and punishment of the wrongdoers, but it equally strongly emphasizes mercy, kindness, and love. Justice, law, and order are necessary for the maintenance of a social order, but there is also a need for forgiveness to heal the wounds and to restore good relations between the people. We must keep in mind that as much as we need God's forgiveness for our own sins and mistakes, we must also practice forgiveness toward those who do wrong to us.

37

On Pilgrimage

Dorothy Day

Dear Father Dan Berrigan:
I woke up thinking of you this morning with love and regret at not having been at the First Street Friday meeting—nor on the picket line with you Saturday at Mother Cabrini's hospital on 19th Street. With love, and gratitude too, for all you are doing—for the way you are spending yourself. Thank God, how the young love you. You must be utterly exhausted too, yet you keep going. I feel this keenly because I've been really down and out since August, what the doctor calls a chronic cough and a mild "heart failure," and I chafe at my enforced absence because of a nervous exhaustion which I realize you must often feel, though you are a generation or more younger than I.

But thank God, you are truly bearing the cross, giving your life for others, as Fr. Phil is in cramped cell and enforced idleness, away from all he must crave day and night to do, surrounded by suffering, enduring the clamor of hell itself—he too is giving his life for others.

I cannot tell you how I love you both, and see more clearly how God is using you, reaching the prisoners and reaching the young. Now that I have five great grandchildren and another on the way, I stress the young. They all call you "Dan" and "Phil," but I call you Fr. Dan and Fr. Phil because always you are to me priests and prophets. . .

Non-Resistance

. . . I feel that, as in the time of the Desert Fathers, the young are fleeing the cities—wandering over the face of the land, living after a fashion in voluntary poverty and manual labor, seeming to be inactive in the "peace movement." I know they are still a part of it—just as Cesar Chavez and the Farm Workers' Movement is also part of it, committed to non-violence, even while they resist, fighting for their lives and their families' lives. (They, together with the blacks, feel and have stated this, that birth control and abortion are genocide.)

I agree with them and say—make room for children, don't do away with them. Up and down and on both sides of the Hudson River religious orders own thousands of acres of land, cultivated, landscaped, but not growing food for the hungry or founding villages for the families or schools for the children.

How well I understand that biblical phrase "in peace is my bitterness most bitter." How to reconcile this with Jesus' new commandment of nonresistance, of loving others, forgiving others seventy times seven—forgiving and loving the enemies of our own household?

Once a monsignor, a generous donor to the CW [Catholic Worker], on hearing of one of our dear and poverty-stricken friends about to have her sixth child, said, "Not much self-control there!"

Another time I went with one of our CW mothers of eight children to the large rectory of the parish to ask that the parish St. Vincent de Paul Society help out with the rent and prevent the eviction of this family of ten. The young mother weeping said, "There is not much food in the house, either." The old pastor grunted, "You don't look as tho you've been going hungry!" She had lost her figure with much childbearing, and from finishing up the scraps the children left, as poor mothers do. But no steaks, salads, fruits, and cheese—not to speak of wines and liqueurs—on the tables of the poor.

Yes, "in peace is my bitterness most bitter." Yet the bitterness subsides and the peace in my heart grows, and even a love and some understanding grows of these "enemies of our own household."

Parables

I must tell little stories, as Jesus taught us to do in trying to teach. They call it "reminiscing," when you are old. I do not undervalue my wisdom, which my age (I begin my 76th year) and experience have taught me.

The story is this. We had a mean pastor once long ago who was always blasting women in his sermons for sitting around gossiping, not cleaning their houses, and spending their husband-soldiers' pay on beer and movies. It was during the Second World War. And there was a man in our house of hospitality arrested for indecent exposure. The parish neighbor who told me this called it "insulting a child," and I had thought she said "assaulting" and nearly fainted with fear and trembling. With no one else to turn to, I went to the pastor, the rigid and cranky one, and asked him to go to the jail, visiting the prisoner being one of the seven corporal works of mercy.

With no comment at all but with the utmost kindness and the delicacy of few words, he did as I requested and interceded for this man off the road and got him a lighter sentence of sixty days. When this happened once again some years later, another priest, a saintly well-spoken one, was appealed to. He is reported to have responded, "Too bad they don't give him a life sentence!"

You never can tell! But there are still, thank God, plenty of priests. One can shop around, though it was not encouraged by those once known as our "spiritual advisers." Perhaps they were right. Priests and laymen educate one another over the years. Besides, in the country one is stuck with one or two.

Besides—I believe. I believe in reading Scripture, studying it. And in this case, taking to heart the story of the importunate widow and the unjust judge, and the friend who made a tumult at the home of his friend, demanding help. Keep asking for help.

I hope we do not lose many subscribers because of my writing so frankly about usually unreferred to portions of our anatomy. But nowadays when there are no longer lines at the confessionals in our churches except at the business district's noonday Masses, there surely is an overflowing of public confessions. In our newspapers, reviews, advertisements, and novels "nothing is hidden it seems, that has not been revealed." It is as tho the fear of death, and judgment day has made people rush to tell all, to confess to each other, before the Dread Judge shall tell all to the universe. Poor, fearful creatures that we are, is it that in this strange perverse way of confessing we are seeking Christ, even those who deny him? Jesus Christ is our truth. By telling the truth, or one aspect of the truth, perhaps we are clinging to the hem of his garment, seeking to touch it like the woman with the "issue of blood," so that we may be healed.

Christ Is Truth

I am not wandering, in writing this way. I am meditating. I am thinking of what I have come to think of as fundamental to our search for peace, for nonviolence. A flood of water (and Christ is living water) washes out sins—all manner of filth, degradation, fear, horror. He is also the Word. And studying the New Testament, and its commentators, have come in this my seventy-sixth year, to think of a few holy words of Jesus as the greatest comfort of my life.

"Judge not."

"Forgive us our trespasses as we forgive those who trespass against us."

"Forgive seventy times seven times."

All words of our Lord and Savior. "I have knowledge of salvation thru forgiveness of my sins," Zacharias sang in his canticle.

And so, when it comes to divorce, birth control, abortion, I must write in this way. The teaching of Christ, the Word, must be upheld. Held up though one would think that it is completely beyond us—out of our reach, impossible to follow. I believe Christ is our Truth and is with us always. We may stretch toward it, falling short, failing seventy times seven, but forgiveness is always there. He is a kind and loving judge. And so are ninety-nine percent of the priests in the confessional. The verdict there is always "not guilty" even though our "firm resolve with the help of his grace to confess our sins, do penance and amend our lives" may seem a hopeless proposition. It always contains, that act of contrition, the phrase "to confess our sins," even though we have just finished confessing them, which indicates that the priest knows, and we know, and we want to be honest about it, that we will be back in that confessional, again and again.

I believe in the sacraments. I believe grace is conferred thru the sacraments. I believe the priest is empowered to forgive sins. Grace is defined as "participation in the divine life," so little by little we are putting off the old man and putting on the new.

Actually, "putting on Christ."

. . . And dear Dan, Fr. Dan, please excuse my wandering like this.

38

Forgiveness Is an Attribute of the Strong

Helen Phillips, MM

It is impossible to live on this planet today without getting hurt and misunderstood, lied to and rejected. Learning how to respond properly is one of the basics of Christian life. In today's world aching from disasters, climate change, opioid epidemic, immigrant children caged in detention centers, crimes, injustices in court cases, racism of many kinds, poverty, corrupt politics on many levels, we have much to deplore, to be angry about. What *will we*, what *can we*, do about this?

St. Matthew 6:5–15 has much to tell us in this regard. Jesus had been going about Galilee preaching to the people. Some of his disciples went aside with him and asked him to teach them how to pray. He didn't give them a formula to recite but began his teaching by saying: "Do not imitate the hypocrites who like to pray where people can see them." They had their reward. Jesus then said, *"When you pray go to your private room and when you have shut the door pray to your Father who is in that secret place; and your Father, who sees all that is done in secret, will reward you. Your Father knows what you need before you ask him; so you should pray like this,"* and it was then that Jesus taught them what we call the Our Father or the Lord's Prayer. This is one of the first prayers we learn as children. It is said in so many languages, throughout the world. We know that prayer so very well! . . . or DO WE? Do we know what it demands of us? After saluting our God as Father we ask for our daily bread which we receive in the Eucharist, and then come the words, some of the most compelling words, that demand our fulfillment and promise us a treasure in return, a remedy for all the troubles mentioned above:

Forgive us our trespasses (sins) as we forgive those who trespass (sin) against us!

Do we ever really forgive? Do we ever really forget a grievance held against us? This demands strength, courage, and humility. Mahatma Gandhi once said: *"The weak can never forgive. Forgiveness is the attribute of the strong,"* while Nelson Mandela, who suffered so very much, said: *"When a deep injury is done to us, we never heal until we forgive."*

Here is the remedy that helps us to meet the challenges before us. Jesus, our Savior, while dying unjustly on the cross, gives us the perfect remedy with which to meet any challenge in this life when he says,

"Father, forgive them, as they know not what they do."

"Yes, if you forgive others their failings, your heavenly Father will forgive you yours. But if you do not forgive theirs, your Father will not forgive your failings either."

Mercies

I did a lot of things that I regretted and I certainly paid for my mistakes. You have to go and ask for forgiveness and it wasn't until I really started doing good and doing right, by other people as well as myself, that I really started to feel that guilt go away. So I don't have a problem going to sleep at night.

—Mark Wahlberg

Who you are is not what you did. You're still an innocent.

—Taylor Swift

I think tolerance and acceptance and love is something that feeds every community.

—Lady Gaga

39

Be Compassionate

Mary Lou Kownacki

When they found the body of five-year-old Lila in a dumpster, my friend Sister Mary Miller told me, "I'm afraid if I met the murderer, I'd want to tear his heart out." She probably voiced the sentiments of most of the city of Erie, Pennsylvania. For fourteen days the entire city had searched for Lila. She had occupied the front page of the Erie newspapers. All places of business, buses, and telephone poles were blanketed with posters of her innocent, smiling face. Churches and synagogues had offered special prayers for her safety.

The morning after the child's badly decomposed body was discovered, the phone rang at our priory. Mary, who is director of our soup kitchen and food pantry, was called to the phone. "Sister Mary, it's me, George. I've got to see you right away."

"The minute I heard his voice I knew it concerned Lila," Sister Mary said. George and his three boys lived across the street from Lila's family. They were two poor families eking out an existence in a tough neighborhood. Minutes after the phone call, Sister Mary was in George's home, trying to be present to a father who had volunteered at Emmaus pantry and whose son was charged with the unimaginable crime. George asked Sister Mary to accompany him to jail that afternoon, "to give my son some spiritual help."

Less than twenty-four hours after she had threatened to rip his heart out, Sister Mary sat facing seventeen-year-old Scott. The accused murderer was not a faceless stranger but a boy she knew—a teenager who had accompanied his father to the pantry a few times. "I needed as much spiritual help as he did," Sister Mary confided. "My heart was full of anger and rage."

According to Mary, her meeting with Scott went something like this: "This is very difficult for me, Scott," she said. "I don't know what to say to you. If this charge is true, then what you've done is a terrible thing, an act most people find unforgivable. All I can do is to tell you about the God I believe in, the God I pray to. That God, Scott, has promised to forgive the most terrible crimes, provided we are sorry. If you killed little Lila, her family may never forgive you, and maybe they shouldn't. Your family, friends, and neighbors might not forgive you either. God, however, is a different story. I don't know if you pray, Scott, but if you did this, then sometime today get down on your knees and beg forgiveness. If you are truly sorry, God will forgive you. Please remember that. Do you understand?" The boy merely nodded and stared vacantly ahead.

"I don't believe cheap forgiveness is a solution," Sister Mary said to me later. "Anger in this case is a justifiable emotion and people like Lila's family and myself have to work through it. If we lie about the anger and mouth words of easy forgiveness, it only means we will act out the pain in other ways.

Anyway, it was the best I could do. I certainly believe in a God of unlimited forgiveness and compassion, but it was a stark reminder of how far I am from the Scripture "Be compassionate as your God is compassionate."

40

Conversion of the Heart

Jim Forest

How dare we hope for God's mercy if we ourselves refuse to be merciful? How can we love someone whom we refuse to forgive? It's not possible. Love of enemies and the willingness to forgive are bound together. The insistence on forgiveness is a basic element of Christ's teaching.

The Greek verb used in the Our Father for "forgive," *aphiemi*, means simply to let go, set aside, or leave behind. The verb, understood in its Greek sense, reminds us that forgiveness is, like love, not a feeling but an action involving our will rather than our emotions. But such a letting go never comes easy, not even for so great a saint as the apostle Peter. On one occasion he put the question to Jesus, "Lord, how many times must I forgive my brother or sister who has sinned against me?" Surely, Peter seems to be saying, there must be a limit. He asks if seven times would not be enough. Jesus answered, "I tell you, not seven times, but seventy times seven" (Matthew 18:21–22).

One of the desert saints of the early church, Abbot Moses the Black, found a dramatic way of proclaiming this gospel principle. He was once asked to take part in a community meeting at which a certain lax brother was to be condemned and perhaps expelled from the brotherhood, but Abbot Moses was reluctant to attend. When he at last arrived, he was carrying a tattered reed basket on his back from which sand was pouring through many openings. "Why are you doing that?" he was asked.

"My sins are running out behind, and I do not see them, and today I come to judge the sins of another!"

The embarrassed community was moved to pardon their brother.

As Saint Moses' simple action bore witness, nothing is more fundamental to Jesus' teaching than his call to forgiveness and mercy: giving up debts, letting go of grievances, pardoning those who have harmed us. It's an element in the one prayer Jesus taught his disciples. Every time we say the Lord's Prayer, we remind God that we ask to be forgiven only insofar as we ourselves have extended forgiveness to others:

"And forgive us our trespasses as we forgive those who trespass against us" (Matthew 6:12; Luke 11:2–4).

A few verses later in Matthew's Gospel, Jesus' teaching on this point continues: "Judge not, that you be not judged. For with the judgment you pronounce you will be judged, and the measure you give will be the measure you get. Why do you see the speck that is in your brother's eye, but fail to notice the log that is in your own?" (Matthew 7:1–3).

This lesson is at the heart of Jesus' parable of the servant whose king forgave him a huge debt, but who afterward refused to forgive the small debt owed to him from a lesser servant and had the man imprisoned. The outraged king says to the unforgiving man: "You wicked servant! I forgave you all that debt because you besought me. Should you not have mercy on your fellow servant as I had mercy on you?" (Matthew 18:32–33).

It's not hard to identify with the reprimanded servant. Who doesn't know how much easier it is to ask God to forgive us than to extend forgiveness to others?

In the eucharistic liturgy of the Orthodox Church, the most frequent response to the many petitions included in the litanies is "Lord have mercy." This appeal for God's forgiveness is repeated countless times at every service.

I know few people for whom forgiveness—being merciful—isn't a day-by-day challenge. We have been wounded, and the wounds often last a lifetime and even spill across generations. As children, as parents, as husbands or wives, as families, as workers, as jobless people, as church members, as members of certain classes or races, as voters, as citizens of particular nations, we have been violated, targeted, lied to, used, abandoned. Sins, often serious sins, have been committed against us. We may feel damaged, scarred for life, stunted. People we love—children, spouses, friends—may even have died of evil done to them. In my own family I often think of my stepmother, Karla, shot dead as she stood waiting for a bus in San Francisco. Every family has its tragic stories.

But we are not only victims with just cause to be angry. In various ways we are linked to injuries others have suffered and are still suffering. If I allow myself to see how far the ripples extend from my small life, I will discover that not only in the places I inhabit and work but on the far side of the planet there are people who are among my victims. Through what I have done or failed to do, through what my community has done or failed to do, there are others whose lives are more wretched than they might have been. The inexpensive shirt I bought—or blouse you bought—may have been made by a woman laboring for meager pay in a firetrap in Pakistan.

We feel justified in condemning the evils we see in others while excusing and justifying the evils we're responsible for ourselves; our own sins, it seems, are much more defensible than theirs. In the area of enmity, we fail to realize that those who threaten us feel threatened by us, and often have good reasons for their fears.

Enmity is often rooted in the unwillingness to forgive.

The problem is not simply a personal issue, for the greatest sins of enmity are committed en masse with very few people feeling any personal responsibility for the violence or destruction they share in doing or preparing. "I was only following orders" is one of humanity's most frequently repeated justifications for killing, heard as often from those who profess religious convictions as from those who deny them.

My friend Hildegard Goss-Mayr tells a remarkable story of a step toward forgiveness that occurred in Poland ten years after the end of World War II. By then the division of Europe had become iron-hard, a nuclear arms race was under way, and the Cold War was getting colder by the day. In Warsaw to take part in a conference, she and her husband, Jean Goss, met privately one evening with a group of Poles to discuss the Stalinist regime that had been imposed on their country, the possibilities for giving nonviolent witness together whenever human rights were violated, and the possibility of collaboration in peacemaking between Poles and Germans:

Defying a law prohibiting group meetings, we met in a flat with some twenty young intellectuals, all committed Christians. It was their first opportunity to meet Christians from the West. The exchange was profound and sincere. It was already late when Jean and I decided to ask a question that was very much on the minds of many young West Germans we knew. . . . "Would you be willing," we asked, "if the possibility should arise, to meet with Christians from West Germany? They want to ask forgiveness for what Germany did to Poland during the war and to begin to build a new relationship." There was a silence. Finally one of our Polish friends, a young writer, jumped up and vehemently said, "Jean and Hildegard, we love you, you are our friends but what you are asking is im-

possible! Each stone of Warsaw has been soaked in Polish blood. We cannot forgive!"

We tried to insist: "Who should make the first step? The nonbelievers? The Communists? Someone else? Or we who are baptized in the name of the One who pardoned the sin of all humanity and overcame hatred through the gift of his life?" But our Polish friend said this was impossible. "This is not yet the time for forgiveness."

Even after a decade, the war wounds remained fresh and deep. Jean and I saw we could go no further. It was getting late. Before separating, we proposed that we recite together the prayer that unites us all, the Our Father. All joined in willingly. But when we got to the passage, "and forgive us our sins as we forgive . . . ," our Polish friends halted in the prayer.

Into this silence the one who had said, "it is impossible," spoke up in a low voice: "I must say yes to you. I could no more pray the Our Father, I could no longer call myself a Christian, if I refuse to forgive. Humanly speaking, I cannot do it, but God will give us his strength!"

It was at that point that all of us understood that peacemaking is impossible without conversion of the heart.

We continued to talk and plan. A year-and-a-half later, after more moderate leaders had replaced the Stalinists, ten of our Polish friends who had been in that room were given visas that allowed them to take part in a meeting in Vienna, the first East–West [International Fellowship of Reconciliation] conference after the war, and here they met with the Germans. From this meeting, many initiatives in East–West relations began. The friendships and consequences continue until today.

Think of this story the next time you recite the Our Father.

We often hear the phrase "forgive and forget." But must true forgiveness imply a willingness to forget? Clearly there is no benefit in hanging on to the memory of trivial events. It's good advice to forget them. But there are events that it would be a sin to forget. As the Orthodox theologian and scholar Metropolitan Kallistos Ware has written,

It would not be right to say to the members of the Armenian nation, "Forget the massacres of 1915," or to the Jewish people, "Forget the Shoah in the Second World War." These are matters that, for the sake of our shared humanity, none of us should forget, not least so as to ensure that such atrocities may never be allowed to happen again. . . . Remember the past but do not be held captive by it. Turn it into a blessing, not a curse; a source of hope, not humiliation. Our memories are not to be repressed or negated, but at the same time they require to be purified and healed. We need to remember . . . in a spirit of compunction and mourning. We need to remember with love. . . . Forgiveness is not primarily our human action but a divine action in which we humans participate.

Yes, I am sometimes reminded, forgiveness is a wonderful thing. But what about anger? Haven't I a right to my anger? When I am hurt, should I pretend not to feel the hurt? And if I manage to hide my hurt and anger, am I not lying?

How easy it is to become an anger-centered, anger-driven person, but it's a condition that solves no problems and makes many worse. Saint Gregory of Nyssa, one of the most revered theologians of the early church, saw the anger that lies behind the refusal of forgiveness as self-destructive: "In condemning your neighbor, you thereby condemn yourself." In a similar vein, the American writer Mark Twain remarked, "Anger is an acid that can do more harm to the vessel in which it is stored than to anything on which it is poured." A comparable insight is attributed to the Buddha: "Anger, like a forest fire, burns up its own support."

Anger and fear are often intertwined—anger a suit

of armor in which fear is hidden. Anger has its place, but it's best if it resembles the brief flame topping a matchstick rather than a permanent volcanic inferno. We see anger in Jesus' life but only in brief flashes. He was furious with those who made a house of worship into a place of thieves; he denounced those who laid on others heavy burdens they did not carry themselves. If you want to see Jesus angry, read the twenty-third chapter of Matthew's Gospel.

Yes, anger can have its place, while a forgiveness that is pretended, that attempts to hide pain and rage behind pretty wallpaper, is of no value. Sooner or later we will discover that our complaints are still there, still fresh, perhaps more explosive than ever. Until we allow ourselves to feel the hurt and to express it, it is unlikely that a genuine act of forgiveness will be possible.

If the pardon we seek to offer to those who need our forgiveness is to be of any use to them, they need to be aware of what they have done and the pain or hurt it has caused. How can they know it if we are silent? Jesus teaches that we have the obligation to speak out: "Take heed to yourselves; if your brother sins, rebuke him, and if he repents, forgive him" (Luke 17:3). Where sincere regret is lacking, one's forgiveness of the other is incomplete—freeing for oneself but shrugged off by the other.

A flash of anger—the sort of anger that the Jesuit poet Daniel Berrigan describes as "outraged love"—may help the other person to realize the gravity of the sin he or she has committed and open the path toward forgiveness. But until we have allowed ourselves to get beyond anger, to forgive, or rather to let God's forgiveness flow through us, we are burdened with our injuries and complaints every bit as much as the ghost of Jacob Marley was held captive by chains and money boxes in Charles Dickens's Christmas Carol.

We are called to forgive. We need to seek forgiveness, offer forgiveness, and accept forgiveness. We are followers of Jesus who taught us forgiveness even when his hands were nailed to the wood of the cross: "Father, forgive them. They know not what they do" (Luke 23:34).

41

Forgive the Inexcusable

C. S. Lewis

We say a great many things in church (and out of church too) without thinking of what we are saying. For instance, we say in the Creed "I believe in the forgiveness of sins." I had been saying it for several years before I asked myself why it was in the Creed. At first sight it seems hardly worth putting in. "If one is a Christian," I thought, "of course one believes in the forgiveness of sins. It goes without saying." But the people who compiled the Creed apparently thought that this was a part of our belief which we needed to be reminded of every time we went to church. And I have begun to see that, as far as I am concerned, they were right. To believe in the forgiveness of sins is not so easy as I thought. Real belief in it is the sort of thing that easily slips away if we don't keep on polishing it up. We believe that God forgives us our sins; but also that he will not do so unless we forgive other people their sins against us. There is no doubt about the second part of this statement. It is in the Lord's Prayer, it was emphatically stated by our Lord. If you don't forgive you will not be forgiven. No exceptions to it. He doesn't say that we are to forgive other people's sins, provided they are not too frightful, or provided there are extenuating circumstances, or anything of that sort. We are to forgive them all, however spiteful, however mean, however often they are repeated. If we don't we shall be forgiven none of our own.

Now it seems to me that we often make a mistake both about God's forgiveness of our sins and about the forgiveness we are told to offer to other people's sins. Take it first about God's forgiveness, I find that when I think I am asking God to forgive me I am often in reality (unless I watch myself very carefully) asking him to do something quite different. I am asking him not to forgive me but to excuse me. But there is all the difference in the world between forgiving and excusing. Forgiveness says, "Yes, you have done this thing, but I accept your apology; I will never hold it against you and everything between us two will be exactly as it was before." If one was not really to blame then there is nothing to forgive. In that sense forgiveness and excusing are almost opposites. Of course, in dozens of cases, either between God and man, or between one man and another, there may be a mixture of the two. Part of what at first seemed to be the sins turns out to be really nobody's fault and is excused; the bit that is left over is forgiven. If you had a perfect excuse, you would not need forgiveness; if the whole of your actions needs forgiveness, then there was no excuse for it.

But the trouble is that what we call "asking God's forgiveness" very often really consists in asking God to accept our excuses. What leads us into this mistake is the fact that there usually is some amount of excuse, some "extenuating circumstances." We are so very anxious to point these things out to God (and to ourselves) that we are apt to forget the very important thing; that is, the bit left over, the bit which excuses don't cover, the bit which is inexcusable but not, thank God, unforgivable. And if we forget this, we shall go away imagining that we have repented and been forgiven when all that has really happened is that we have satisfied ourselves with our own excuses. They may be very bad excuses; we are all too easily satisfied about ourselves. There are two remedies for this danger.

One is to remember that God knows all the real excuses very much better than we do. If there are real "extenuating circumstances" there is no fear that he will overlook them. Often he must know many excuses that we have never even thought of, and therefore humble souls will, after death, have the delightful surprise of discovering that on certain occasions they sinned much less than they thought. All the real excusing he will do. What we have got to take to him is the inexcusable bit, the sin. We are only wasting our time talking about all the parts which can (we think) be excused. When you go to a doctor you show him the bit of you that is wrong, say, a broken arm. It would be a mere waste of time to keep on explaining that your legs and throat and eyes are all right. You may be mistaken in thinking so, and anyway, if they are really right, the doctor will know that.

The second remedy is really and truly to believe in the forgiveness of sins. A great deal of our anxiety to make excuses comes from not really believing in it, from thinking that God will not take us to himself again unless he is satisfied that some sort of case can be made out in our favor. But that is not forgiveness at all. Real forgiveness means looking steadily at the sin, the sin that is left over without any excuse, after all allowances have been made, and seeing it in all its horror, dirt, meanness, and malice, and nevertheless being wholly reconciled to the man who has done it.

When it comes to a question of our forgiving other people, it is partly the same and partly different. It is the same because, here also forgiving does not mean excusing. Many people seem to think it does. They think that if you ask them to forgive someone who has cheated or bullied them you are trying to make out that there was really no cheating or bullying. But if that were so, there would be nothing to forgive. (This doesn't mean that you must necessarily believe his next promise. It does mean that you must make every effort to kill every taste of resentment in your own heart—every wish to humiliate or hurt him or to pay him out.) The difference between this situation and the one in which you are asking God's forgiveness is this. In our own case we accept excuses too easily, in other people's we do not accept them easily enough. As regards my own sins it is a safe bet (though not a certainty) that the excuses are not really so good as I think; as regards other men's sins against me it is a safe bet (though not a certainty) that the excuses are better than I think. One must therefore begin by attending to everything which may show that the other man was not so much to blame as we thought. But even if he is absolutely fully to blame we still have to forgive him; and even if ninety-nine per cent of his apparent guilt can be explained away by really good excuses, the problem of forgiveness begins with the one per cent of guilt that is left over.

To excuse, what can really produce good excuses is not Christian charity; it is only fairness. To be a Christian means to forgive the inexcusable, because God has forgiven the inexcusable in you. This is hard. It is perhaps not so hard to forgive a single great injury. But to forgive the incessant provocations of daily life—to keep on forgiving the bossy mother-in-law, the bullying husband, the nagging wife, the selfish daughter, the deceitful son—how can we do it? Only, I think, by remembering where we stand, by meaning our words when we say in our prayers each night, "Forgive our trespasses as we forgive those that trespass against us." We are offered forgiveness on no other terms. To refuse it is to refuse God's mercy for ourselves. There is no hint of exceptions and God means what he says.

A Mercy

Anna Karenina

"But if it is repeated?"

"It cannot be, as I understand it . . ."

"Yes, but could you forgive it?"

"I don't know, I can't judge . . . Yes, I can," said Anna, thinking a moment; and grasping the position in her thought and weighing it in her inner balance, she added: "Yes, I can, I can, I can. Yes, I could forgive it. I could not be the same, no; but I could forgive it, and forgive it as though it had never been, never been at all . . ."

"Oh, of course," Dolly interposed quickly, as though saying what she had more than once thought, "else it would not be forgiveness. If one forgives, it must be completely, completely. Come, let us go; I'll take you to your room," she said, get-

ting up, and on the way she embraced Anna. "My dear, how glad I am you came. It has made things better, ever so much better." (1.19.50)

Anna argues that she could forgive repeated infidelity, and would forgive it as though it never happened. Dolly replies that that's the only kind of forgiveness there is. But do you believe Anna? Maybe she could forgive Karenin if he were unfaithful to her, since she doesn't love him anyway. But could she forgive Vronsky if he cheated on her? After all, in the last parts of the novel, Anna is consumed with jealousy over Vronsky. What do you think?

—Leo Tolstoy

42

The Forgiveness of Sin

Joan Chittister

Perhaps forgiveness is the last thing mentioned in the Creed because it is the last thing learned in life. Perhaps none of us can understand the forgiveness of God until we ourselves have learned to forgive. Perhaps we cannot understand the goodness of God to us because we are so seldom that good to others. On the contrary, we want mercy for ourselves but exact justice for the remainder of humankind. God, on the other hand, the Creed implies, desires justice but gives mercy like a rushing river, gushes mercy like a running stream.

Forgiveness, perhaps the most divine of the divine attributes, ranks, as well, as the most basic of human processes, the one that really brings us to the zenith of ourselves. To forgive is to be like God. God the Forgiver stands before us, beckoning us to holiness, showing us forgiveness as the way to wholeness: to mental health, to personal growth, to independence of emotions, to freedom of soul. Among Jesus' last words on the cross are words of forgiveness. Jesus—come to the fullness of humanity, the end time, the final moment—goes burned into our mind as a forgiver. Clearly, to be everything we can become, we must learn to forgive.

But there are two kinds of forgiveness: one healthy, one not. One is of God, the other a kind of holy affectation, a game we play on ourselves in the name of holiness and wonder why it doesn't work. Forgiveness only works when we are as aware of what vengeance does to ourselves as we are of what it does to the other.

Forgiveness implies two options: We can forego the right to requital or we can simply choose to forego payment of a just debt. We can let go of resentment and the expectation of retribution or, in a gust of moral superiority, simply be generous enough to dismiss the obligation of the debtor. But not the debt. We cease to demand repayment but, down deep, we never forget that payment is still owed.

To forego repayment for harms done releases the debtor but continues to hold us captive to the uncompensated debt, continues to eat away at the inside of us forever. We keep the debtor in spiritual servitude and ourselves in hostile chains. If all we do is to accept the fact that there will be no repayment coming for the harm that was done to us and make the best of a bad thing, the debt remains. Always there, never satisfied. We ourselves are never free of it.

But the failure to forgive, the unyielding memory of the debt, is too great a burden to carry. It smothers the joy out of life. It blocks our own ability to move. It makes growth impossible. It traps us in the juices of the snake that bit us. That is not the mercy of the forgiving God who wipes out the past and, every day, makes all things new again. To forego the need for requital releases us as well as our debtor from further harm. We free the debtor from shame and ourselves from bitterness.

And do not be misled. The Creed is clear about the situation. The Creed is talking about forgiveness for sin, real sin, not merely the invalidation of some kind of gross but basically benign misunderstanding. Harm has been done. Trust has been betrayed. Goodness has been foresworn for personal advantage. Someone has, like Cain, ceased to be my keeper and slain my heart. Then forgiveness, not dissembling, is imperative.

This violation of ourselves is not about social formality. This is about relationships rent. This is about repair. This is about the need for real forgiveness, not cheap forgiveness, the kind counseled for the sake of a false peace. "Oh, don't let it bother you" is not an answer to sin. "Just don't pay any attention to it" does not erase the pain in the heart. "Just forget it. Put it down" dismisses both the sinner and the sinned-against. It asks for tawdry, cocktail-party forgiveness, for "niceness" that fails to diminish the pain, that leaves the sore raw but covered over by the cosmetics of civility waiting to erupt again. This is not the kind of forgiveness that makes for peace, either between people or between nations.

Real forgiveness relies, like the forgiveness of God, on full acknowledgment of the act that impaled the heart of a person, full knowledge of the motive, full acceptance of the human condition: People do these things. It is not so much what a person does to us that is the essence of forgiveness. It is what we do because of the sorrow we suffer that counts.

Premature forgiveness doesn't work. All it does is to substitute formality where genuine connection should be. It leaves the process of forgiveness incomplete. It risks the possibility of submerging feelings that will only rise again in us, displaced perhaps but there nevertheless, until we embrace them, face them, and, perhaps still smarting from the blow of them, move on beyond what cannot be changed to another point in life. Then, all the ruptures can be repaired and forgiveness can be total because the fruits of sin have finally come to full. Not because they were good but because we went beyond them. That is divine forgiveness, the awareness that though evil has been done, the spirit is whole.

This prayer found by the side of a dead child at a concentration camp at the end of World War II may tell it all:

O Lord,
Remember not only the men
and women of goodwill,
But all those of ill will.
But do not remember all the suffering
They have inflicted upon us;
Remember the fruits we have brought
Thanks to this suffering—
Our comradeship, our loyalty, our humility,
Our courage, our generosity,
the greatness of heart
Which has grown out of all of this;
And when they come to judgment,
Let all the fruits which we have borne
Be their forgiveness. Amen.

It is only when we forgive that peace comes. When we suppress the pain that comes from sin, when we seek retribution rather than a new beginning, then the evil of vengeance and the failure of forgetfulness reproduce evil in abundance, repeat evil everywhere.

The Sufi, Imam Husayn, called the king of martyrs, said: "Nobility is to choose forgiveness when revenge is in your power."

It is easy to talk of perfection. It is commonplace to talk of union with God. It is simple to varnish over feelings with propriety. But to reach to the heights of the Creed, to believe in forgiveness and so to be forgiving, now that is difficult. Until we know what it is to forgive the other, to walk beyond the crush of hurt and live again, holding no grudges, requiring no retribution, seeking no compensation, to liberate the sinner from the weight of the sin, we can never understand the forgiveness of God. More, we may never ourselves put on the heart of God. The Creed leaves us with the image of a God for whom forgiveness is of the essence and from whose love we are all bound to learn.

If anything proves the Godness of Jesus, if anything calls us to the divine in ourselves, if anything inspires belief, surely it is the words on the cross that beg forgiveness for the unforgivable. Now, for our own sake, as well as the sake of the rest of the world, it's our turn to forgive.

43

The Miracle of Forgiveness

Marianne Williamson

There are two basic filters through which to view all things: the filter of the body, and the filter of the spirit. To the extent that you view your life only through the body's filter, you are bound to the body in a way that does not serve you. Being bound to the body, you are at the effect of the body's appetites, whether they are healthy or dysfunctional. But when your eyes are lifted, giving you the capacity to see beyond the body to the realm of spirit, you're given power over your body that otherwise you do not have. Dwelling lightly within your body, your body becomes light.

And how do you do that? How do you see beyond the body? You do it by being willing to extend your focus beyond the dramas of the material plane, remembering that beyond this drama there is the truer truth of who we all are. What is love is real, and what is fear is mere illusion. Yes, a friend might have said something cruel to you—but in her heart, she's simply lost and lonely like everyone else. Your friend does love you; she was just disconnected from her love at the moment when she made that comment. It helps to remember that whatever trauma you experienced in your childhood was probably not all that different from what other people experienced in theirs.

No matter what happens to you, you have a choice as to how to interpret it. You will make that choice—consciously or subconsciously. You can focus on the body's drama—your friend's hurtful words, her mistake, her betrayal. But if you do, you won't be able to escape the emotional experience of being at the effect of her words. By choosing to focus on the material drama, particularly the drama of guilt, you increase your attachment to the material plane and thus your vulnerability to its dysfunctions. You forgive because you wish to stay above the dramas of the material world, particularly the drama of your addiction.

Your alternative choice is to focus on the innocence in your friend—on her divine reality that is beyond, and truer, than her bodily self. All of us are made of love, yet all of us make mistakes. In detaching from an overemphasis on someone else's mistakes, you detach from an overemphasis on your own. As you reach across the wall of separateness—and there is no wall thicker than the wall of judgment—then the wall comes down. That is the miracle of forgiveness.

Forgiveness is selective remembering, a conscious choice to look beyond guilt to innocence. In common parlance, it usually amounts to simply cutting people more slack. This serves you. Judgment and blame put stress on the body of whoever is doing the judging and blaming, and stress is the time bomb at the center of your addiction. It is in "staying above" the drama of the body that you dwell more harmoniously within it. Your body was not created to bear the burden of your overattachment to it, but was created as a container for the light of your spirit. It will more easily remember how to function perfectly when you remember the perfection in everyone.

As you forgive others, you begin to forgive yourself. As you stop focusing on their mistakes, you will stop punishing yourself for your own. Your ability to release what you think of as the sins of others will free you to release yourself, putting down the weapon with which you punish yourself so savagely. Forgiveness releases the past to divine correction and the future to new possibilities. Whatever it was that happened to you, it is over. It happened in the past; in the present, it does not exist unless you bring it with you. Nothing anyone has ever done to you has permanent effects, unless you hold on to it permanently.

Dear God,
Please teach me to forgive
myself and others.
Remove the walls
that keep love out,
behind which I am prisoner.
Heal my guilt
and remove my anger,
that I might be reborn.
Make gentle my heart
and strong my spirit,
and show me how to love.
Amen

Sources and Acknowledgments

Orbis Books has made every effort to identify the owner of each selection in this book, and to obtain permission from the author, publisher, or agent in question. In the event of inadvertent errors, please notify us.

1. Anne Lamott, "The Gentle Gift of Mercy," excerpted from "The Mercy Workshop," in *Hallelujah Anyway: Rediscovering Mercy* by Anne Lamott. Copyright © 2017 by Anne Lamott. Used by permission of Riverhead, an imprint of Penguin Publishing Group, a division of Penguin Random House LLC, and The Wylie Agency LLC. All Rights reserved.

2. Jack Kornfield, "Forgiveness Repairs the World," published as "A Psychology of Virtue, Redemption, and Forgiveness," in T*he Wise Heart: A Guide to the Universal Teachings of Buddhist Psychology* by Jack Kornfield. Copyright © 2008 by Jack Kornfield. Used by permission of Bantam Books, an imprint of Random House, a division of Penguin Random House LLC. All rights reserved.

3. Mary Oliver, "A Settlement," from *What Do We Know: Poems and Prose* by Mary Oliver. Copyright © 2002 by Mary Oliver. Reprinted by permission of Da Capo Press, an imprint of Hachette Book Group, Inc.

4. Jon Mundy, *"The Key to Happiness,"* from Miracles Magazine, Nov/Dec 2009. Reprinted by permission of Jon Mundy.

5. Frederick Buechner, "The Freedom to Be at Peace," from *Wishful Thinking: A Theological ABC.* New York: Harper & Row, 1973. Reprinted by permission of Frederick Buechner Literary Assets, LLC.

6. Henri Nouwen, "Giving and Receiving," from *Bread for the Journey: A Daybook of Wisdom and Faith.* Copyright © 1997 by Henri J. M. Nouwen. Reprinted by permission of HarperCollins Publishers.

7. Eric Immel, SJ, "I Want You Back: On Asking for Pardon," from *The Jesuit Post*, May 31, 2017. Reprinted by permission of Eric Immel, SJ.

8. Robert J. Wicks, "Failure and Forgiveness of Yourself," for *The Way of Forgiveness: Readings for a Peaceful Life*. Maryknoll, NY: Orbis Books, 2019. Used by permission of Robert J. Wicks.

9. Quang Trí, "Buddha's Lesson on Forgiveness," from BuddhaJourney.net, April 15, 2013.

10. Simcha Fisher, "The Comedy of Confession," from *America Magazine*, March 22, 2018. Reprinted by permission of Simcha Fisher.

11. Pierre Eau Claire, "Beyond Ideas," original poem for *The Way of Forgiveness: Readings for a Peaceful Life*. Maryknoll, NY: Orbis Books, 2019.

12. e. e. cummings, "a total stranger one black day." Copyright © 1957, 1985, 1991 by the Trustees for the E. E. Cummings Trust, from *Complete Poems: 1904–1962* by E. E. Cummings, edited by George J. Firmage. Used by permission of Liveright Publishing Corporation.

13. James Martin, SJ, "They Do Not Know What They Are Doing," from *Seven Last Words* by James Martin, SJ. Copyright © 2016 by James Martin, SJ. Reprinted by permission of HarperCollins Publishers.

14. Kim Phuc, "The Long Road to Forgiveness," from *This I Believe II: More Personal Philosophies of Remarkable Men and Women*, edited by Jay Allison and Dan Gediman. Copyright © 2008 by Kim Phuc. Copyright © 2008 by This I Believe, Inc. Reprinted by permission of Henry Holt and Company. All Rights Reserved.

15. Ron Rolheiser, "Forgiveness Is the Only Thing That Is New in the World," from ronrolheiser.com 4/13/98. Used by permission of Ron Rolheiser.

16. Joyce Rupp, "Sour Memories," original poem for *The Way of Forgiveness: Readings for a Peaceful Life*. Maryknoll, NY: Orbis Books, 2019. Used by permission of Joyce Rupp.

17. Lynn F. Monahan, "So, I Opted to Go for It," an interview with

Ocan Robert Venderiko from *Maryknoll* magazine, July/August 2018.

18. Michael Leach, "Antoinette Bosco—Model of Forgiveness," from *Why Stay Catholic?* by Michael Leach. Loyola Press, 2011. Copyright © 2011 by Michael Leach. Reprinted with permission of Loyola Press. To order copies visit www.loyolapress.com.

19. David Steindl-Rast, OSB, "Love Your Enemies! What Does It Mean? Can It Be Done?" Originally published on gratefulness.org, © A Network for Grateful Living.

20. Victor Parachin, "Practicing the Fine Art of Forgiveness," from *Eastern Wisdom for Western Minds*. Maryknoll, NY: Orbis Books, 2007.

21. Pierre Eau Claire, "Meanest," original poem for *The Way of Forgiveness: Readings for a Peaceful Life*. Maryknoll, NY: Orbis Books, 2019.

22. Richard Rohr, "The Power of Forgiveness," from *Hope Against Darkness: The Transforming Vision of Saint Francis in an Age of Anxiety* by Richard Rohr with John Feister. Copyright © 2001 by Richard Rohr, O.F.M., and John Feister. Published by Franciscan Media. Reprinted by permission of Franciscan Media.

23. Douglas Venne, MM, "An Attitude of Heart," from *What They Taught Us: How Maryknoll Missioners Were Evangelized by the Poor*, Joseph A. Heim, MM, editor. Maryknoll, NY: Orbis Books, 2009.

24. Guy de Maupassant, "It's Never Too Late," short story first published in 1882, reprinted from www.americanliterature.com.

25. Harold Kushner, "Forgiveness Is a Favor We Do Ourselves," Jewels of Elul website, September 19, 2017. Reprinted by permission of Rabbi Harold Kushner.

26. Brian Doyle, "The Day I Stood Simmering in Shame," from *National Catholic Reporter* (January 2014). Copyright © 2014 by Brian Doyle. Reprinted with the permission of The Permissions

Company, Inc., on behalf of the Estate of Brian Doyle, www.permissionscompany.com.

27. Joan Chittister, "What Kind of People Are These?" *National Catholic Reporter,* October 9, 2006. Reprinted by permission from Benetvision, Erie, PA.

28. Alice Camille, "Punched in the Stomach," excerpt from a talk by Alice Camille. Used by permission of Alice Camille.

29. Maya Angelou, "Forgive" from *I Shall Not Be Moved* by Maya Angelou, copyright © 1990 by Maya Angelou. Used by permission of Random House, an imprint and division of Penguin Random House LLC, and Little, Brown Book Group Ltd., London. All rights reserved.

30. Michael Leach, "Forgiveness Is the Only Way to Begin," originally published by *National Catholic Reporter*, NCRonline.org, April 9, 2013. Reprinted by permission of National Catholic Reporter.

31. Henri Nouwen. "The First Step of Forgiveness," from *Forgiveness: The Name of Love in a Wounded World*, by Henri Nouwen, is reprinted here with the permission of the Henri Nouwen Legacy Trust.

32. Gerald G. Jampolsky, "The Miracle of the Butterfly," from www.servingyourjourney.com.

33. Julie Schumacher Cohen, "The Plus Sign," from *America Magazine,* March 15, 2018. Reprinted by permission of Julie Schumacher Cohen.

34. Metropolitan Anthony of Sourozh, "Forgiveness Sunday," Sermon at Vespers, Forgiveness Sunday, March 16, 1986. Reprinted by permission of the Metropolitan Anthony of Sourozh Foundation.

35. William F. Mullan, MM, "Jesus Challenges Us," from *What They Taught Us: How Maryknoll Missioners Were Evangelized by the Poor,* Joseph A. Heim, MM, editor. Maryknoll, NY: Orbis Books, 2009.

36. Muzammil Siddiqi, "God the Forgiver: Forgiveness and Repentance in Islam," from IslamiCity, April 17, 2018. Used by permission of islamicity.org.

37. Dorothy Day, "On Pilgrimage," first published in *The Catholic Worker*, December 1972.

38. Helen Phillips, MM, "Forgiveness Is an Attribute of the Strong," for *The Way of Forgiveness: Readings for a Peaceful Life.* Maryknoll, NY: Orbis Books, 2019. Used by permission of Helen Phillips.

39. Mary Lou Kownacki, "Be Compassionate," from *A Monk in the Inner City: The ABCs of a Spiritual Journey*. Maryknoll, NY: Orbis Books, 2008.

40. Jim Forest, "Conversion of the Heart," from *Loving Our Enemies: Reflections on the Hardest Commandment*. Maryknoll, NY: Orbis Books, 2014.

41. C. S. Lewis, "Forgive the Inexcusable," from *The Weight of Glory* by C. S. Lewis, copyright © C. S. Lewis Pte. Ltd. 1949. Extract reprinted by permission of C. S. Lewis Company.

42. Joan Chittister, "The Forgiveness of Sin," from In Search of Belief Liguori, MI: Liguori Publications, 2006. Used with permission. All rights reserved, Liguori.org.

43. Marianne Williamson, "The Miracle of Forgiveness," from www.healyourlife.com. Used by permission of Marianne Williamson.

Index of Contributors

Rediscovering Mercy. She is also a well-known political activist, public speaker, and writing teacher. **1**

Michael Leach is publisher emeritus of Orbis Books. A leader in Catholic publishing for more than forty years, he has edited and published more than three thousand books. In 2007, the Catholic Book Publishers Association honored him with a Lifetime Achievement Award. **18, 30**

C. S. Lewis (d. 1963) was an Anglican writer and theologian. He was known for both his spiritual writings, including *Mere Christianity and Miracles*, and his works of fiction, including *The Screwtape Letters* and *The Chronicles of Narnia*. **41**

James Martin, SJ, is a Jesuit priest, an editor at *America* magazine, and a well-known American spiritual writer. His most recent book is *Building a Bridge: How the Catholic Church and the LGBT Community Can Enter into a Relationship of Respect, Compassion, and Sensitivity*. In 2017, Orbis Books published a collection of many of his written works, *James Martin: Essential Writings*. **13**

Guy de Maupassant (d. 1893) was a French naturalist fiction writer. He wrote more than 300 short stories, six novels, three travel books, and one volume of poetry. **24**

Lynn F. Monahan is editor-in-chief of *Maryknoll magazine*. He served as a Maryknoll lay missioner in Peru in the 1990s. His novel *Pistaco* was published in 2017. . . . . **17**

William F. Mullan, MM, is a Maryknoll priest who spent almost four decades as a missionary in Guatemala. He also served as Mary knoll's U.S. regional superior from 1991 to 1997. . . . . **35**

Jon Mundy is an author, lecturer, and the publisher of *Miracles* magazine. He was a co-founder of The New Seminary for Interfaith Ministers in 1981. His nine books include *Living a Course in Miracles*. . . **4**

Henri Nouwen (d. 1996) was a Dutch Catholic priest and one of the most popular spiritual writers of the twentieth century. He was the author of more than forty books, including *The Wounded Healer* and *Adam: God's Beloved*. **6, 31**

Index of Contributors